Catholic Mosaic

Living the Liturgical Year with Literature:
An Illustrated Book Study for Catholic Children

Cay Gibson
Edited by Rose Decaen

Hillside Education
475 Bidwell Hill Road
Lake Ariel, PA 18436

www.hillsideeducation.com

Cover image reprinted by permission of Art Resource, Inc.
>
> *Saint Anne and the Virgin* by Bartolome Esteban Murillo
> Photo credit: Erich Lessing/Art Resource, NY

Original art by Sean Fitzpatrick: Mother Teresa, John Paul II, *Song of the Swallows, The Giving Tree, The Blackbird's Nest, The Tale of Three Trees,* and the monthly images.

Original art by Maureen Van Nostrand: page borders, Ethiopian Cross, Princess' Kiss, and *Little Rose of Sharon,* and *St. Francis and the Christmas Donkey.*

Lay out by Mary Jo Loboda

Book design by Margot Davidson

Grateful acknowledgement is made to the publishers and artists who granted us permission to use reprints of their book covers. Credits listed in order of appearance in this book.

Mary Joslin/Alison Wisenfield, *Mary: Mother of Jesus* (London, UK: Lion Hudson, pcl and Chicago: Loyola, 1999).

Han Christian Anderson/Rachel Isadora, *The Little Match Girl* (New York, NY: Penguin Books for Young Readers, 1987).

Fredrick H Thury/Vlasta van Kampen, *The Last Straw* (Watertown, MA: Charlesbridge Publishing, 1998) Text copyright" 1998 Fredrick H Thury, Illustrations copyright"1998 by Vlasta van Kampen. Used with permission by Charlesbridge Publishing Inc. All rights reserved.

Susan Brindle/Ann Brindle/Margaret Brindle, *The Most Beautiful Thing in the World* (New Hope, KY: Precious Life Books Inc., 2004).

Bryce Milligan/Helen Cann, *Brigid's Cloak* (Grand Rapids, MI: Eerdmans, 2005).

Susan Brindle/Ann Brindle/Maragaret Brindle, *Children's Stations of the Cross* (New Hope, KY: Precious Life Books, Inc., 1997).

Margaret Hodge/Trina Schart Hyman, *St. George and the Dragon* (New York, NY: Little, Brown Publishers, 1984).

Susan Andrews Brindle/Miriam Andrews Lademan, Joan Andrews Bell, *The Little Caterpillar that Finds Jesus* (Precious Life Books, Inc., 1999).

Josephine Nobisso/Katalin Szegedi, *The Weight of a Mass: A Tale of Faith* (Westhampton, NY: Gingerbread House, 2002).

Irene Hooker/Susan Andrews Brindle/Miriam Andrews Lademan, *The Caterpillar that Came to Church* (Huntington, IN: Our Sunday Visitor, 1993).

Joan Bell/Susan Brindle/Miriam Lademan, *Lovely Lady Dressed in Blue* (Precious Life Books, Inc., 1994).

Margaret Hodge/Richard Jesse Watson, *The Legend of Saint Christopher* (Grand Rapids, MI: Eerdmans, 2002.

Wendy Goody and Veronica Kelly/Ginny Pruitt, *A Peek into My Church* (Los Altos, CA: Whippersnapper Books, 1997.

Elizabeth Loch, *Juanita and Our Lady of the Angels* (New Hope, KY: New Hope Publications, 2001).

Jan Cheripko/Kestutis Kasparavicius, *Brother Bartholomew and the Apple Grove* (Honesdale, PA: Boyds Mills Press, 2004).

Marybeth Lorbiecki.Wendy Popp, *Sister Anne's Hands* (New York, NY: Penguin Books for Young Readers, 2000).

Regina Doman/Ben Hatke, *Angel in the Waters* (Manchester, NH: Sophia Institute Press, 2004).

Miriam Lademan/Susan Brindle, *My Guardian Dear* (New Hope, KY: Precious Life Books, Inc, 1996).

Susan Andrews Brindle/Miriam Andrews Lademan, *Father Phillip Tells a Ghost Story: A Story of Divine Mercy* (New Hope, KY: Precious Life Books, Inc., 1996).

Lesbia Scott/ Judith Gwyn Brown, *I Sing a Song of the Saints of God* (New York, NY: Morehouse Group, 1994) Permission to reprint granted by the artist. The original illustrations for this book are in the permanent collection of the Boston Public Library.

Janice Levy/Morella Fuenmayer, *The Spirit of Tio Fernando: A Day of the Dead Story* (Morton Grove, IL: Albert Whitman, 1995).

Augustine Denoble/Judith Brown, *Brother Joseph, Painter of Icons* (Bathgate, ND: Bethlehem Books, 2000).

Tomie DePaola, *Clown of God* (New York, NY: Harcourt Books, 1978).

Gloria Whelan/Judith Brown, *The Miracle of Saint Nicholas* (Bathgate, ND: Bethlehem Books, 2000).

Barbara Helen Berger, *The Donkey's Dream* (New York, NY: Penguin Books for Young Readers, 1985).

This book is dedicated to my beautiful daughters and goddaughters—the girls who make my life as rich and colorful as a Mosaic:

Kayleigh, Chelsea, Annalice, Ashleigh, Megan, Lynsey, Kaitlynn, Rebecca, Abigail, and Rachel
—**C.G.**

Go, little Book; from this my solitude,
I cast thee on the waters:—go thy ways!
And if, as I believe, thy vein be good,
The World will find thee, after many days.
Be it with thee according to thy worth:—
Go, little Book! in faith I send thee forth.
—Robert Southey

Foreword

There is a growing box of books and assorted curricular materials in the large walk-in closet that is our home library. In it, materials I have purchased but no longer use (or may have never used) are being gathered to sell or donate. For now, though, it stands as a staunch reminder not to buy, sight unseen, every good idea about which I read. Often, one person's good idea becomes my bookend. Instead, when purchasing curriculum, it is better for me to sit here one day—or maybe for several weeks—and think to myself, "I wish there were a book that did . . . "

For more years than I can count, I have thought, "I wish there were an organized way to integrate the Liturgical Year, great literature, notebooking, copywork, simple crafts, and Catechesis of the Good Shepherd." Such a project was daunting. In order to pull it off, one would have to be immersed in living the Liturgical Year. One would have to spend hours researching the wealth of beautiful religious picture books available out there "somewhere." One would have to have a grasp on the concept of notebooking and a sense of how the faith is taught in a Montessori atrium. Then, one would have to make the time to put it all together in a useable format. Some of us dreamed of such a resource. One of us did it.

Cay Gibson, together with Hillside Education, has done a masterful job of creating a lovely, living mosaic of literature-based catechesis—a Catholic Mosaic.

When a child learns the faith within the context of the Liturgical Year, "religion" becomes a living, breathing part of the rhythm of life. It is integrated into her being as fundamentally as a heartbeat. In early December, she just *knows* it is Advent; that's the way it's always been. She thinks, "Our color is purple because we are waiting, preparing." She looks forward to celebrating the feasts that are nestled in among the fast. St. Nicholas, Juan Diego, Our Lady of Guadalupe, St. Lucy—all her favorite, familiar friends are met with joy. And when she is older, she will not merely turn the calendar to the last month of the year inside a dry, secular cubicle, she will instead continue to live the richness of the first season of the Church year. And if, for some sad reason, she does not, something will seem terribly out of sync, for that will not be the normal, habitual beating of her heart from the beginning when she was a child in the Domestic Church of her parents.

When the faith is taught within the context of living books a lyrical song is sung, a beautiful image embossed upon a child's soul. Those carefully chosen books become family traditions. "This is the book we read for St. Brigid's feast; this for John Paul II's birthday; this for Pentecost." Children learn the stories of the saints and they develop real, living relationships with those holy men and women who cheer them from heaven and intercede on their behalf. The saints of those stories are faithful friends for small children who grow into spiritual giants and guides for well-formed adults. The books Cay has chosen are of the highest quality—living, breathing books that will infuse children and the adults who share them with the breath of the Holy Spirit.

When notebooking is introduced to the teaching of religion and academia meets theology in the context of the rhythm of the household, you have real learning. No one can tell where "school" stops and "church" begins, where "church" stops and family life begins. Instead, there is a lifestyle of learning within the heart of the Domestic Church. It is education within the bosom of the family, just as the Creator intended. Catholic Mosaic offers a plethora of ideas for organizing just such an education. It's all tied together and keyed to the calendar. We can do this! We can have an environment in our homes that is this rich and meaningful!

There will be no used copies of this resource available. Mothers who forego home education to send their children to school will hold on to this book in order to read the stories at bedtime and do the crafts on rainy Saturdays. Mothers whose children have grown and gone will pass the book to their daughters and daughters-in-law. It is a resource destined to become dog-eared and jelly smeared.

At 4Real, we've embraced this resource with great zeal. We are talking about it. We are adding more books and more ideas and we archiving the success stories. Come join us. We are piecing together a life in our homes that is reminiscent of a mosaic in a fine cathedral—something truly rich and beautiful for our Lord.

—Elizabeth Foss
Author of *Real Learning in the Heart of the Home*

Acknowledgements

Putting together a book is a special kind of creative artwork. Since art can be a form of prayer, each endeavor contributed here was indeed a prayer lifted upward for the greater glory of God. And the prayers were many.

As no man is an island, neither is a book one person's contribution alone. The author of *Catholic Mosaic* wishes to express her heartfelt thanks to many people who helped bring the pieces of this book together and create the finished mosaic.

—To editor, Rose Decaen, for tirelessly going through page after page, taking all the broken pieces of art and turning them into a literary mosaic; also for taking on the necessary job of contacting publishers to obtain reprint rights on book covers.

—To Mary Jo Loboda for setting the mosaic into its final mold so carefully and elegantly.

—To artists Sean Fitzpatrick and Maureen Van Nostrand, whose creative styles and artistic endeavors put the grace and creative flair into the final product.

—To the online communities of Real Learning (www.4reallearning.com) and Literature Alive! (http://groups.yahoo.com/group/LiteratureAlive/) who have strewn the many colorful book tiles found in this Mosaic onto my path through the years.

—And to my publisher, Margot Davidson, at Hillside Education who immediately took this project under her wing with enthusiasm and shared vision. Without her, this Mosaic would be missing many pieces of tile. She is the mortar that held it all together. The simple words "thank you" fail to convey my sincere appreciation for all she has done.

*****

I would be remiss if I did not extend a special thank you to Elizabeth Foss for showing me how captivating illustrated books could be and how to use them in my home. Also, thanks are due to Regina Doman for putting the term *"renaissance of children's literature"* into my head. This simple term became the framework for the entire mosaic.

—Cay Gibso

No man is an island, entire of itself
very man is a piece of the continent, a part of the main.
If a clod be washed away by the sea,
Europe is the less, as well as if a promontory were,
as well as if a manor of thy friend's or of thine own were.
—John Donne (1573-1631)

Notes from the Author

A Renaissance of Children's Literature

Catholic author Regina Doman introduced me to the phrase "A renaissance of children's literature" a couple years before *Catholic Mosaic* came into being. The term intrigued and captured my imagination. After all, the word "renaissance" means *rebirth*. It is never too late to give birth within our homes to the rich world of children's literature and, in doing so, to recapture the loveliness these books offered us in our childhood. Even the simplest picture books can bear fruit in the lives of young and old alike. And so, I began to look at picture books with a more discerning eye. What I saw pleased my senses, my imagination, my children, and my home.

During this time, I was working through the Catholic Church's liturgical year with my children. We had started a Liturgical Year Notebook and were using the Liturgical Year Calendar Coloring Kit purchased from Our Father's House. (See Recommended Resource section at the end of this introduction.) I was also using Moira Farrell's *Home Catechesis Manuals* (for use with the *Catechesis of the Good Shepherd* method, also available from Our Father's House) to develop an atrium[1] within my home. So I began searching for illustrated books to read to my children about our Catholic faith, the saints, and Church history.

I didn't have to look far. Emmanuel Books and Catholic Heritage Curricula offered many worthy books. Then I found a delightful *Collection of Children's Catholic Literature* made available at WhipperSnapper Books. (See Recommended Resource section.) And we began to fill the liturgical year within our domestic church with lots of amazing books that enriched our faith and blessed our family.

Illustrated books work marvelously well with children. Children do not relate well to abstract concepts. That is why God has always been drawn as an old man with a long white beard. That is why angels are drawn with bodies and wings. That is why the Holy Ghost is shown as a dove descending from heaven. Children need the visual and the concrete in order to examine, study, and understand the abstract. As a matter of fact, we all do! That is why we light candles on our birthday cake to mark each year of our life. That is why Christ comes to dwell in us under the appearance of bread and wine. That is why the beautiful Catholic Church has always used water and oil and incense and candles

---

[1] Definition of *atrium:* a spiritual setting where the Montessori method of "self-teaching" is used in a classroom setting or, in the case of a home setting, as a prayer corner. It is often referred to as "holy ground" and, in the words of Catechesis of the Good Shepherd foundress, Gianna Gobbi, "creates the conditions for silence and reverence and helps children focus on and listen to God."

and scapulars and statues and all the other accolades of worship. We are visual beings. We have both a spiritual side and a physical side. We need the concrete here on earth to remind us of the spiritual realities.

For the younger children, these books are prayers that can be lifted up and could be read at the same time that bedtime prayers are recited. I have found them worth culling with my older children as well since they are short, enjoyable reads.

This text supplies you with a complete reading list of illustrated books with Catholic themes that you and your child can use to celebrate the liturgical year. The selected titles are perfect for enriching your child's sacrament preparation and your family's feast day observances. You may want to purchase a liturgical calendar wheel or make one yourself to follow the year of the Church. (See resource section.)

The author's ongoing vision is to help parents and educators see the value and purpose in good quality picture books (our little ones need no convincing!). They are treasures well worth returning to and re-exploring. I hope you will find within this guide a *mosaic art print* that will color your family's home and lives in years to come.

Happy reading!

Ad Maiorem Dei Gloriam
—Cay Gibson, January 2006
cajuncottage.blogspot.com

Introduction

What is the *Catholic Mosaic*?

Catholic Mosaic is a book study of various Catholic illustrated books that are brought together into a design which illustrates the whole liturgical year. It is a gentle attempt to help the parent and child recapture the beauty of our Catholic faith and explore the *renaissance of catholic children's literature* that we are so fortunate to be a part of. Discussion questions, vocabulary words, copy work, activities, and observations are offered for the parent to use with their child after one reading of the book.

Catholic home educating parents today have an amazing array of curriculum choices. In an attempt to cram it all in, we become overwhelmed. We lose the joy of the moment and forget the wonder of learning—all because we are so busy doing too much. We lose our focus. This literary study is not intended to be one more thing to *cram* into your schedule. You'll see that this is a simple program—one that a parent can simply pick up and use at leisure. Families who are not home educating will also be able to easily add these discussions to their story book time. The books should take no more than 15-20 minutes to read. Some families might find it best to read the story and discuss it after morning prayers around the breakfast table; others will prefer reading at bedtime after nightly prayers.

The time spent with these illustrated classics should be a thought-provoking, treasured time that you share with your children. Use this opportunity to help them fall in love with the Kingdom of God. That is what the *Catholic Mosaic* seeks to do: to enable parents and children to find wonder and joy in these illustrated books. It is suggested that parents read the guide pages before reading the book to their child. Then pick up the book and explore it to understand it, wander in it to find the wonder, reflect upon it to sense God's reflection in yourself, and talk about it to find the joy. You and the book are God's instrument in passing God's message to your child. Allow the Holy Spirit to work through the language and art work of the story. Have faith in your child to understand the story and digest it. Experience the book fully, yet with compassion, richness, and grace.

Do I need to purchase the individual titles studied in *Catholic Mosaic*?

No, although all of these beautiful books would make a great addition to your personal collection, you can easily borrow them from the local library. If your local library does not have a particular title, make a book request. Every library has a book budget so help them spend it!

If your church has a lending library, check with the pastor or Director of Religious

Education about purchasing some of these titles for the younger children. If your church doesn't have a library, look into getting one started. If all else fails consider giving your children some of these books as Christmas, birthday, and/or feast day gifts. Many of the titles may be purchased from Sacred Heart Books and Gifts (www.sacredheartbooksandgifts.com) and Emmanuel Books (www.emmanuelbooks.com). A list of suppliers has been included on page 18.

Please note: Some titles are, sadly, out of print. Be on the lookout for them at books sales and online.

Are any supplemental materials required in the *Mosaic*?

No. The illustrated books are the main focus of this guide and are stand-alones. But the author has used supplements within her home which have proven to be immeasurably beneficial to the program. For the sake of sharing these resources with other Catholic parents, the author is including them in the Recommended Resource section at the end of this introductory material.

Can *Catholic Mosaic* be used as a catechetical program?

Catholic Mosaic is not meant to replace your parish's CCD program, although this literary study can reinforce and supplement those programs through visual artwork and language. The stories in *Catholic Mosaic* connect the child to matters of faith, spiritual figures, and moral truths in a way that textbooks cannot. We hope that Catholic Mosaic will draw children closer to the beauty, richness, and color of Holy Mother the Church; and that, through these beginnings, children will have a greater desire to learn about the Catholic faith and its traditions and history as they grow older.

Are these all Catholic books?

While some books like Hans Christian Andersen's *The Little Match Girl*, Dan Brown's *Across a Dark and Wild Sea*, and Bryce Milligan's *Brigid's Cloak*, are not, strictly speaking, Catholic stories, they have been included in the *Mosaic*. If you look deep into the heart and soul of these books, you will see why they were selected:

> Finally, brethren, whatever is true, whatever is honorable,
> whatever is just, whatever is pure, whatever is lovely,
> whatever is gracious, if there is any excellence, if there is
> anything worthy of praise, think about these things.
> —St. Paul's Letter to the Phillipians 4:8

They are all, as St. Paul exhorts, true, honorable, just, pure, lovely, and/or gracious works.

We need to teach our children to have an objective eye and, as the late Pope John Paul II showed us so wonderfully well by his example, to see the truths of their faith in the world around them. Let the Holy Spirit guide you in your discussions with your child, praying that the things we dwell upon lead us to heaven.

If you have any concerns about one of the books, set aside 15 minutes to review the book before sharing it with your child.

While we have attempted to place the books in the most appropriate place in the liturgical calendar, you may choose to read the books at the time of year you feel is best. For example, *The Tale of Three Trees* by Angela Elwell Hunt could have been placed either in the Easter or the Christmas season. However, in observance of the Feast of the Exaltation of the Cross, we placed it in September.

You will find the spring months full of books on the sacraments since that is when three of our sacraments are most often received (Penance, First Communion, and Confirmation), but they can be read at any time of the year.

For what age group is *Catholic Mosaic* intended?

This program will appeal primarily to children of kindergarten age through fourth grade. These books can be read to children of all ages but it has been the author's experience that K-4th graders receive it best.

A few of the books, such as *Sr. Anne's Hands*—which focuses on racial discrimination— are in some ways better suited for upper elementary level students. Still there is nothing objectionable in these books for younger students. They won't necessarily understand the events of racial segregation, but they will learn something about prejudice and why it is hurtful and un-Christian.

How do I use *Catholic Mosaic*?

It is suggested that the parent set aside one half-hour each week to read, review, and discuss each book with his/her child. Discussion questions and vocabulary words (as well as a "Parent's Help" page) have been supplied. In addition, for some books there are enrichment activity suggestions, copywork assignments, and observations. Use as few or as many of these extra activities as fits your family schedule.

Student Activities for Each Book

Vocabulary Words
Go over the vocabulary words with your child to make sure he/she understands

them. Providing oral explanations of the vocabulary words is very helpful. Let the child define the words he/she knows. If there is a word he/she does not know, gently give the definition. When you come across the word in the text, remind your child of the definition. Then with the definition fresh on his/her mind, reread the sentence.

Discussion Questions

The discussion questions are designed to foster conversation between parent and child. After reading the story with your child, ask him/her the discussion questions. Allow your child to answer the questions. Do not attempt to answer the questions for him/her, and do not incorporate a test format into your discussion session. Remember, the questions are intended to be used as conversation starters. (The questions possibly add an extra 5-10 minutes to your reading time.)

Copywork

This is a special line or phrase from the book or from Scripture which bears repeating and memorizing. At some point, have your child copy the line or phrase into a prayer journal, a copy notebook, or onto the designated activity project. These lines could also be included in the liturgical notebook. (Not every book has a copywork assignment. For those weeks, you might look for a Scripture verse for the child to copy.)

Parent's Help Page

On this page the parent is given more information about the story and activity suggestions to extend the ideas in the story.

Observation

These are suggestions for you to make sure your child practices an objective eye in observing and discerning clues within the story. They may also include special things that the illustrator designed to add richness or extra information to the story.

Discussion Answers

Some suggested answers for the questions are given for the parent.

Enrichment Activities

These are simple and doable activities that reinforce the message found in the story. There is little to no preparation work for the parent. The child may do the activity some time during the week. Some of the activities direct the student to look up the setting of the story on a map. Please see the Appendix for a collection of maps that you may use to mark the location of places in the stories.

Liturgical Year Notebook

If a parent would like to "enshrine" any copy work, art projects, or narrated essays of their child's, we suggest making a Liturgical Year Notebook. These are relatively easy to make and can be added to in future years.

Our Liturgical Year Notebook is a one-inch binder divided into categories. Using color-coded labels, we make the following categories:

> Religion Clock (Liturgical Year Wheel – see resources
> section)
> Advent
> Christmas
> Epiphany
> Lent
> Easter
> Pentecost
> Ordinary Time
> Baptism
> Penance
> First Communion
> Confirmation
> Vocations
> Saints
> Rosary
> Mary
> Pope

Some of our display material became too massive, demanding that we transfer the work into a single folder with packets and brads. These folders, when finished, are placed safely in our Liturgical Notebook.

We have found that Catholic Heritage Curricula's materials lend themselves extremely well to notebook inclusions. The ideas found in their lesson plans (memory cards, faith sheets, and homemade booklets) work well in completing your Liturgical Year Notebook.

(See the Resource Section for ordering information.)

Reading Graph and Book Stickers

This is an optional "fancy-style" reading chart with book stickers that help motivate young readers. As the child completes the reading of a book, he may apply a sticker to the reading chart. For more information on this resource, please contact the author at caygibson@gmail. com. .

Recommended Resources
Listed Alphabetically

1. **Adoremus Books**
   Frederick Square Shopping Center
   2992 S. 84th St.
   Omaha, NE 68124
   888-392-1973
   http://www.adoremusbooks.com/

   A wide collection of books for Catholic families.

2. **Aquinas and More Catholic Goods**
   1-866-428-2820
   http://www.aquinasandmore.com/

   A wide collection of Catholic books and gifts as well as digital resources, informative podcasts, and lively discussion.

3. **Catholic Heritage Curricula (CHC)**
   Phone: 800-490-7713
   www.chcweb.com

   You will find many hands on activities for the liturgical year at this website. CHC's book *A Year with God* is particularly useful and includes instructions for making a liturgical wheel. Activities from *A Year with God* that complement *Catholic Mosaic's* book study are listed in the Appendix.

4. **Catholic Montessori**
   1090 Payne Avenue
   Saint Paul, MN 55101
   Phone: 1-800-588-2589
   http://www.catholicmontessori.com/

   This is a great Internet location for finding Montessori-oriented information and products. There you will find a message board, a photo gallery, and an online store supplied with items suitable for beginning an atrium within your home.

5. **Emmanuel Books**
   P.O. Box 321
   New Castle, DE 19720
   Phone: 800-871-5598
   www.emmanuelbooks.com

   Emmanuel Books carries many of the books included in *Catholic Mosaic*, as well as a host of other educational resources.

5. **Our Father's House**
5530 S. Orcas St.
Seattle, WA 98118
Phone: 206-725-0461

www.ourfathershouse.biz

Parents who want to make this literature study come more "alive" for their child, might look into investing in Moira Farrell's wonderful *Home Catechesis Manuals*. These manuals have proven to be a rich linkage in our home. They are a Montessori, hands-on, step-by-step, paged workshop designed for the Catholic family. The albums are pricey but not near what the price of a Montessori program would cost the family's budget. A mother need not take a Good Shepherd Catechesis instructor class if she has these books at her disposal.

Our Father's House also carries several good reference books about children and their religious experience and implementing the Good Shepherd program:

The Mass Explained to Children by Maria Montessori
The Catechesis of the Good Shepherd in a Parish Setting by Tina Lillig
The Good Shepherd and the Child by Sofia Cavalletti/ Patricia Coulter/ Gianna
    Gobbi/Silvana Q. Montanaro, M.D.
Listening to God with Children by Gianna Gobbi
The Religious Potential of the Child by Sofia Cavaletti
Living Liturgy by Sofia Cavaletti
History's Golden Thread by Sofia Cavaletti

6. **Seton Home Study School**
1350 Progress Drive
Front Royal, VA 22630
Phone: 540-636-9990

http://www.setonhome.org/

Seton's *Art I* activity book is a wonderful resource for the liturgical year and has easy arts or craft activities included for many feast days. See the Appendix for particular activities that can be used with the books in *Catholic Mosaic*.

6. **Sacred Heart Books and Gifts**
14202 Pier Place
Liberty, MO 64068
Phone: 866-415-4301 (Toll Free) or 816-415-4301
www.sacredheartbooksandgifts.com

You will find many Catholic picture books at this site including some of those studied in *Catholic Mosaic*.

Catholic Mosaic

Booklist

This Mosaic covers 52 children books. In the booklist, you will notice a cross emblem next to the book titles that are chosen for inclusion in this study. You may wish to locate those that are not included in this guide to read with your child as well. Special care has been taken to include selected books for every month of the year.

JANUARY

January 1 Feast of Mary, the Mother of God
✝ *Mary: The Mother of Jesus* by Tomie dePaola $30
✝ *Mary: Mother of Jesus* by Mary Joslin/Alison Wisenfeld $16

Twelve days of Christmas
✝ *The Little Match Girl* by H.C. Andersen/illustrated by Rachel Isadora $6

Feast of the Epiphany
✝ *The Last Straw* by Fredrick H. Thury/Vlasta van Kampen $8
Story of the Three Wise Kings by Tomie dePaola $24

January 21 Feast of Our Lady of Altagracia
✝ *A Gift of Gracias* by Julia Alvarez/Beatriz Vidal $1

FEBRUARY

First Confession
✓✝ *The Most Beautiful Thing in the World* by Susan Brindle/ Ann Brindle/ Margaret Brindle

February 1
✓✝ *Brigid's Cloak: An Ancient Irish Story* by Bryce Milligan/ Helen Cann $9
The Life of St. Brigid: Abbess of Kildare by Jane G. Meyer/Zachary Lynch $500 !!

February 10
✝ *The Holy Twins: Benedict and Scholastica* by Kathleen Norris/ Tomie dePaola $15

February 11
Caedmon's Song by Bill Slavin/Ruth Ashby $15

February 14
✝ *Saint Valentine* by Robert Sabuda $7
Love Is... by Wendy Anderson Halperin $12

MARCH

March 17
✓✝ *Patrick: Patron Saint of Ireland* by Tomie dePaola $7
St. Patrick by Ann Tompert/ Michael Garland $5

March 19 Feast of St. Joseph, Spouse of Mary
✝ *The Song of the Swallows* by Leo Politi

March 20
The Ravens of Farne: A Tale of Saint Cuthbert by Donna Farley/Heather Hayward

Lenten Reading
The Story of the Cross: The Stations of the Cross for Children by Mary Joslin/ Gail
     Newey
✝ *Children's Stations of the Cross* by Susan Brindle/ Joan Bell/ Miriam Lademan
✝ *The Giving Tree* by Shel Silverstein

APRIL

Good Friday
✝ *Little Rose of Sharon* by Nan Gurley/ Tim Jonke
Through the Eyes of John by Chad Daybell/Rhett E. Murphy

Easter
✝ *Easter is for Me!* by Dani Daley Mackall
✝ *The Easter Story* by Brian Wildsmith
Petook by Tomie DePaola
The Very First Easter by Paul Maier/Francisco Ordaz

Divine Mercy Sunday
Helen's Special Picture by David Previtali

April 16
Bernadette: The Little Girl from Lourdes by Sophie Maraval-Hutin/ Adeline Avril

April 16 (Pope Benedict XVI's birthday)
Joseph and Chico: The Life of Pope Benedict XVI as Told by a Cat by Jeanne Perego
     by Donata Dal Molin Casagrande and Georg Ganswein
Max and Benedict: A Bird's Eye View of the Pope's Daily Life by Jeanne Perego/
     Donata Casagrande

April 23
The Saint Who Fought the Dragon by Cornelia Mary Bilinsky/ Theresa Brandon
Saint George & the Dragon by Jim Forest/ Vladislav Andrejev
✝ Saint George and the Dragon by Margaret Hodges/ Trina Schart Hyman

Adoration of the Blessed Sacrament
✝ *The Little Caterpillar that Finds Jesus: A Parable of the Eucharist* by Susan Andrews
     Brindle/Miriam Andrews Lademan/ Joan Andrews Bell

MAY

First Holy Communion

✓☩ *The Weight of a Mass: A Tale of Faith* by Josephine Nobisso/ Katalin Szegedi
☩ *The Caterpillar that Came to Church: A Story of the Eucharist* by Irene Hooker/
      Susan Andrews Brindle/ Miriam Andrews Lademan

May 1st

☩ *Lovely Lady Dressed in Blue* by Joan Bell/ Susan Brindle/ Miriam Lademan
The Lady in the Blue Cloak: Legends from the Texas Missions by Eric Kimmel/
      Susan Guevara
Friendship with Jesus: Pope Benedict Speak to Children on their First Holy Communion
      by Amy Welborn/Ann Kissane Engelhart

May 16

St. Brendan and the Voyage Before Columbus by Michael McGrew/ Marnie Litz

May 17

☩ *Pascual and the Kitchen Angels* by Tomie dePaola

May 18 (Birthday Pope John Paul II)

☩ *Karol from Poland* by M. Leonora Wilson/ Carla Koch
Friday Night with the Pope by Jacque Shore/ Amalia Hoffman

May 30th

Joan of Arc: the Lily Maid by Margaret Hodges/ Robert Rayevsky
Joan of Arc by Diane Stanley
Joan of Arc by Josephine Poole/ Angela Barrett

JUNE

Remembering the Prophets of Sacred Scripture by Marianna Mayer
Tapestries: Stories of Women in the Bible by Ruth Sanderson
The Fish in the Fountain: A Story of Baptism by Susan A. Brindle/ Miriam A. Lademan/
Carmen A. Emmanuelli Klosterman

Courtship and Marriage

☩ *The Princess and the Kiss: A Story of God's Gift of Purity* by Jennie Bishop/
      Preston McDaniels
Little Turtledove Finds His Mate by Miriam Lademan/ Susan Brindle

Pentecost

☩ *The Twelve Apostles* by Marianna Mayer
The Very First Christians by Paul Maier/ Francisco Ordaz

June 3
✝ *The Blackbird's Nest: St. Kevin of Ireland* by Jenny Schroedel/Doug Montross
June 9
✝ *Across A Dark and Wild Sea* by Don Brown

JULY

A Child's Rule of Life by Robert Hugh Benson
The Squire and the Scroll: A Tale of the Rewards of a Pure Heart by Jennie Bishop

July 11
✝ *The Holy Twins* by Kathleen Norris/Tomie DePaola

July 14
Kateri Native American Saint: The Life and Miracles of Kateri Tekakwitha by
      Geovanna Paponetti
Blessed Kateri Tekakwitha by Anne E. Neuberger/ Kevin Davidson
Saint Kateri Tekakwitha by Bernadette Nippert and George and Belinda Nippert.

July 25
✝ *Christopher, the Holy Giant* by Tomie dePaola
✝ *The Legend of Saint Christopher* by Margaret Hodges/ Richard Jesse Watson
✝ *A Peek into My Church* by Wendy Goody and Veronica Kelly/Ginny Pruitt

AUGUST

I Believe: The Nicene Creed by Pauline Baynes
A Child's Book of Prayer in Art by Sister Wendy Beckett

August 2
✝ *Juanita and Our Lady of the Angels* by Elizabeth Loch

August 4
John Mary Vianney The Holy Cure of Ars by Sophie De Mullenheim
Joseph's Hands by Kety Sabatini// Marie Sabatini

August 10 Feast of St. Lawrence, Patron of Cooks
Brother Jerome and the Angels in the Bakery by Dominic Garramone/ Richard Bernal

August 11
Clare and Francis by Guido Visconti/ Bimba Landmann
✝ *Sister Anne's Hands* by Marybeth Lorbiecki/ K. Wendy Popp

August 24
✝ *Brother Bartholomew and the Apple Grove* by Jan Cheripko/Kestutis Kasparavicius

August 27
Stories Told by Mother Teresa by Teresa/Edward LeJoly/ Jaya Chaliha/ Allan Drummond

SEPTEMBER

The Monk Who Grew Prayer by Claire Brandenburg

September 5
✝ *Mother Teresa* by Demi

September 9
✝ *Peter Claver, Patron Saint of Slaves* by Julia Durango/Rebecca Garcia-Franco
St. Ciaran, the Tale of a Saint of Ireland by Gary D. Schmidt/Todd Doney

September 11
The Boy, A Kitchen, and His Cave: The Tale of St. Euphrosynos the Cook by Catherine K. Contopoulos/ Chrissanth Greene-Gross

September 14 Feast of the Exaltation of the Cross
✝ *The Tale of Three Trees* by Angela Elwell Hunt/ Tim Jonke

September 17
The Secret World of Hildegard by Jonah Winter/ Jeanette Winter

September 25
The Wonderful Life of Saint Sergius of Radonezh by Alvin Alexsi Currier/ Nadezda Glazunova

September 30
✝ St Jerome and Lion by Margaret Hodges

OCTOBER

Respect Life Month
✝ *Angel in the Waters* by Regina Doman, Ben Hatke
Horton Hears a Who! by Dr. Seuss

October 1
Therese: The Little Flower of Lisieux by Sioux Berger

October 2
✝ *My Guardian Dear* by Miriam Lademan/Susan Brindle

October 4
Francis: The Poor Man of Assisi by Tomie dePaola
St. Francis by Brian Wildsmith
✝ *The Good Man of Assisi* by Mary Joslin/ Alison Wisenfeld
Francis Woke Up Early by Josephine Nobissco/Maureen Hyde
Brother Sun, Sister Moon by Margaret Mayo/ Peter Malone
Brother Sun, Sister Moon by Katherine Paterson/ Pamela Dalton

October 6
Under the Grapevine: A Miracle by St. Kendeas of Cyprus by Chrissi Hart/
    Claire Brandenburg

October 22
Lolek - The Boy Who Became Pope John Paul II by Mark Hoffman/ Mary Hramiec
    Hoffman

October 27
✝ *A Saint and His Lion, A Tale of Saint Tekla* by Elaine Murray Stone/Cecile Sharratt

October 31
✝ *Father Phillip Tells a Ghost Story: A Story of Divine Mercy* by Susan Andrews Brindle/
    Miriam Andrews Lademan
Moonlight Miracle by Tony Magliano/ Susan Andrews Brindle

NOVEMBER

Election Day--Freedom of Religion
Drita: An Albanian Girl Discovers her Ancestors' Faith by Renee Ritsi/ Cameron Thorp

November 1
✝ *I Sing a Song of the Saints of God* by Lesbia Scott/ Judith Gwyn Brown
Saints: Lives and Illuminations by Ruth Sanderson

November 2
✝ *The Spirit of Tio Fernando: A Day of the Dead Story* by Janice Levy/ Morella
    Fuenmayor

November 3
The Pied Piper of Peru by Ann Tompert/ Kestutis/ Kasparavicius
✝ *Brother Joseph, The Painter of Icons* by Augustine Denoble

November 9 Feast of the Dedication of St. John Lateran
Ambrose and the Cathedral Dream by Margo Sorenson/ Katalin Szegedi

DECEMBER

The Christmas Miracle of Jonathan Toomey by Susan Wojciechowski/ P.J. Lynch
The Gift of the Magi by O. Henry/ Lisbeth Zwerger

Advent Reading
✝ *Saint Francis and the Christmas Donkey* by Robert Byrd
✝ *The Clown of God* by Tomie dePaola
✝ *The Miracle of Saint Nicholas* by Gloria Whelan/ Judith Brown

December 6
Saint Nicholas by Ann Tompert/ Michael Garland
Saint Nicholas: The Real Story of the Christmas Legend by Julie Stiegemeyer/
     Chris Ellison
The Legend of Saint Nicholas by Demi
The Real Santa Claus by Marianna Mayer

December 12
✝ *The Lady of Guadalupe* by Tomie dePaola
✝ *The Legend of the Poinsettia* by Tomie dePaola

December 24
The Night of Las Posadas by Tomie dePaola

Christmas Day/Season
The Very First Christmas by Paul Maier/ Francisco Ordaz
A Small Miracle by Peter Collington
✝ *The Donkey's Dream* by Barbara Helen Berger
✝ *The Crippled Lamb* by Max Lucado/ Liz Bonham

Ordinary Time throughout the Year

For the Children by Pope John Paul II
If Jesus Came to My House by Joan G. Thomas
In the Midst of Chaos, Peace Reflections by Sister Wendy Beckett, art by Sister
     Mary Jean Dorcy/Daniel Thomas Paulos
My Path to Heaven by Geoffrey Bliss/Caryll Houselander
Shoemaker Martin Based on a story by Leo Tolstoy/Bernadette Watts
Take it to the Queen: A Tale of Hope by Josephine Nobisso/Katalin Szeged
A Handshake from Heaven by Carol S. Bannon/ Michaelin Otis
Will You Bless Me? by Neal Lorzano/ Ben Hatke
Brother Juniper by Diane Gibfried/ Meilo So
Journey to the Heart: Centering Prayer for Children by Frank X. Jelenek/ Ann Boyajian
God's House by Ellen Javernick/ Virginia H. Richards & D. Thomas Halpin
Feathers and Fools by Mem Fox/ Nicholas Wilton

Annotated Book List

Christ didn't give theological lectures so much as he told
stories. In reading the gospels intact, we find that the
stories Jesus told resonate with us, as they would have with
his original audience, because they're about people we
recognize—a worker and an employer, guests at a wedding,
a man building a house. More than anything, stories give
us a window through which to understand life and why
it changes. We have a powerful need to be part of a story
larger than ourselves.

> —Sarah Koops Vanderveen in "Storytelling"
> Issue 22 of MARS HILL REVIEW.

Use these annotations as little windows to help you select and preview the 52 books
featured in this guide.

Mary, Mother of Jesus
Written by Mary Joslin/ Illustrated by Alison Wisenfeld
Mary, The Mother of Jesus
Written and Illustrated by Tomie dePaola
Author Mary Joslin tells the story *Mary, Mother of Jesus* as a first person narrative. Mary is an
elderly woman who shares her life story with anyone who will listen…including your child.

Author Tomie dePaola's book tells Mary's story in more detail. It should probably be read and
discussed one passage at a time so your child can fully appreciate the events of Mary's life.

In reading these two books, your child will come to see how Mary was able to fully
accept the grace of becoming the Savior's mother and to embrace the seven swords that
pierced her heart. Realizing Mary's joy at being the Mother of all mankind, your child
will be better able to proclaim with true appreciation, "Blessed art thou among women!"

The Little Match Girl
Written by Hans Christian Andersen/ Illustrated by Rachel Isadora
The Little Match Girl is one of my fondest childhood reads. In the story, an innocent child
longs for comfort, warmth, love, and beauty but is exposed, instead, to harsh conditions,
bitter cold, absence of love, and ugliness. The comfort of home, the warmth of the stove
and roasted goose, the beauty of a Christmas tree, and the loving arms of a grandmother
will touch every heart that lives in this imperfect world yet strives for the ideal vision of
comfort, warmth, love, and beauty that only Heaven and God can give.

The Last Straw
Written by Fredrick H. Thury/ Illustrated by Vlasta van Kampen
The Last Straw by Fredrick Thury is a lovely book. Dear old Hoshmakaka is a weary
old camel plagued by aching joints, gout, and a dreadful sciatica nerve problem. He is

happy to sleep most of the time, compete in water-drinking contests, and attend the local cud-chewing convention. What a relaxed life he leads! Until voices in the desert sand tell him that he has been chosen to "*carry gifts to a baby king.*" And dear old Hoshmakaka grudgingly answers their call.

Every hour on the hour someone blocks his path and asks him to take his/her gift to the newborn king. Complaining of his joints, his gout, his sciatica every step of the way; he slowly makes his way across the desert. When he reaches the manger at last, Hoshmakaka has a beautiful and unexpected encounter with the baby King. It's a Christmas story you simply have to read.

A Gift of Gracias
Written by Julia Alvarez/ Illustrated by Beatriz Vidal
Here is a Marian story that you probably haven't heard. It's based on a true story about an apparition of our Blessed Mother that took place in the Dominican Republic. *Our Lady of Altagracia* (High Grace or Thanks) blesses a farmer and his family with an orchard of oranges, which saves the family's farm. The delightful story and stunning folk art-type pictures will light your way into a study of Marian apparitions.

The Most Beautiful Thing in the World
Adapted from Story by Rev. Gerald T. Brennan/ Illustrated by Susan Andrews Brindle, Ann Gershona Brindle, Margaret Mary Brindle
What a lovely lesson in simplicity! This is the perfect book to read as part of your child's preparation for First Confession. The angels in heaven have instructed a very little angel to go to earth and find *the most beautiful thing in the world.* What will it be? Will it be a beautiful rose? A lovely snow covered mountain? An innocent newborn baby? Your child will discover, and you will too, that all human beings hold the secret to *the most beautiful thing in the world.* It is there for each of us to find, if we only open our heart and soul to Christ and welcome His gift of grace into our lives.

Brigid's Cloak
Written by Bryce Milligan/ Illustrated by Helen Cann
This book shows a small part of St. Brigid's story. Still, it is a way to introduce your child to Brigid, her homeland, and the humble conditions in which she was raised. The story includes a recounting of a mystical experience Brigid had on a cold December night in which she shares her cloak with the Blessed Mother and holds Baby Jesus.

The Holy Twins
Written by Kathleen Norris/ Illustrated by Tomie dePaola
The Holy Twins is a delightful book for all ages. Not much is known about St. Benedict and his sister St. Scholastica, but one can learn the highlights of their lives by reading this simple book by the famed author of The Cloister Walk. Whether you are the roaming traveler, intent on searching for Christ in all the hidden places (like St. Benedict) or whether you're a homebody, content on finding Christ in your own domestic church (like St. Scholastica), this book will show you how we do not find Christ—He finds us.

Saint Valentine
Retold and Illustrated by Robert Sabuda

Legendary historical figures often inspire many lores and legends. So it has been with the romantic figure of St. Valentine. Author Robert Sabuda focuses on one version of this saint's life and lets his carefully chosen text and mosaic-style pictures tell the rest of the story. The artwork in this book makes it a delightful Valentine's Day read.

Patrick, Patron Saint of Ireland
Written and Illustrated by Tomie dePaola

What child hasn't heard the story of St. Patrick and his famous signature emblem, the shamrock? But did you know that St. Patrick also was instrumental in driving the snakes from the emerald isles of Ireland? Did you know that St. Patrick was not originally from Ireland but was brought to Ireland as a slave? This book will surprise many readers who thought they knew the famous saint so well.

Song of the Swallows
Written and Illustrated by Leo Politi

Did you know that the swallows migrate to San Juan Capistrano Mission every year on the feast day of St. Joseph, March 19? Why is that? This little book might lead your child on self-study trails about swallows, bird migration, California missions, and Fr. Junipero Serra. Celebrate the coming of spring with this book that tells about a real life mystery—a mystery that confirms the relationship between the natural and the supernatural.

Children's Stations of the Cross
Written and Illustrated by Susan Andrews Brindle, Joan Andrews Bell, Miriam Andrews Lademan

The Passion of Christ. The Road to Calvary. The Way of the Cross. Via Dolorosa. The Stations of the Cross can be a hard road for some parents to take with their children. This book vividly yet gracefully takes parents and children down that sorrowful journey and reveals to us why we should make the walk, what we gain by it, and how we are called to embrace our own crosses in life. Allow your child the opportunity to observe the pictures during his devotional-prayer time.

The Giving Tree
Written and Illustrated by Shel Silverstein

This book needs no introduction. Thousands of us have already read it—many times. Read it again with your child and see how the Catholic faith can be found in the simplest storybooks, even those about a boy and a tree.

The Easter Story
Written and illustrated by Brian Wildsmith|

In his signature artistic style, Wildsmith colorfully recounts the story of the passion and Resurrection of Jesus Christ. He begins with the triumphant entry into Jerusalem and follows the Bible story faithfully through the Passion. Great book for reading throughout Holy Week and Easter. Read one page a day to tell the story over the course of the week.

Little Rose of Sharon
Written by Nan Gurley/ Illustrated by Tim Jonke

This sweet book will show your child how even the smallest of God's creation can serve the greater good. A rose that resides in the Valley of Sharon takes great pride in being a thing of beauty for the Creator. When a storm propels a tiny dove egg underneath her foliage, she is aware that the baby bird within the egg will never have the gift of life if she does not sacrifice her beauty to shield it. Your child will see the connection between Jesus' sacrifice and that of the little rose.

Easter is For Me!
Written Written by Dandi Daley Mackall/ Illustrated by Anton Petrov

Easter is for Me! is an artistic pleasure as soon as you open the book. The pictures are lovely, colors are vibrant, and facial expressions are real. The script, written in rhyme, repeatedly refers back to the child who is being read the book. It introduces the child through a portion of Christ's life and each page, each beautiful depiction, reminds the child that everything Jesus' did, every step Jesus took, every sermon and parable Jesus spoke was intentionally done for the child who hears the word of God. And it is all part of His mighty, mysterious plan.

St. George and the Dragon
Retold by Margaret Hodges/ Illustrated by Trina Schart Hyman

This book is rich in beautiful art and the reader will find in it an introduction to the world of folklore where good battles evil. Based on Spenser's Faery Tales, a medieval classic, the story involves a beautiful princess who seeks the help of a fearless knight to save her and her homeland from the evil dragon. Given the Catholic symbolism found throughout the story, this book could easily serve as a springboard for further study of Medieval times, knights, and the Crusades. Wonderful for older students to read in preparation for the Sacrament of Confirmation.

The Little Caterpillar That Finds Jesus: A Parable of the Eucharist
Written and Illustrated by Susan Andrew Brindle/Miriam Andrews Lademan/ Joan Andrews Bell

The Andrew sisters have done it again in this beautiful parable of the Holy Eucharist. The main character, Gloriana, is so much like each of us. We find our little niche, our little comfort zone, and we are happy and content. Then someone or something comes along and snatches us out of our happy garden. We suddenly find ourselves out of our comfort zone and left in a panic. We can do nothing but lean on God, pray, and await His will. While we wait, Jesus is working on our hearts, minds, and souls. We hear Him in the silence. We feel Him in the stillness. And we are transformed into the people He wants us to be. This book shows your child the true beauty of Christ present in the Blessed Eucharist. Great for first communion preparation.

The Weight of a Mass, A Tale of Faith
Written by Josephine Nobisso/ Illustrated by Katalin Szegedi
The Weight of a Mass is truly a Catholic masterpiece. Author Josephine Nobisso has combined all the key elements that children look for and love in a story: a fairy-tale setting, a king and queen in a royal kingdom, delectable sweets for a child's sweet tooth, and a satisfying ending. Buy a copy of this book to keep on your shelf. Read it to all your children. Read it by yourself. See for yourself what the weight of a Mass really is.

The Caterpillar That Came to Church: A Story of the Eucharist
Written by Irene H. Hooker/ Susan Andrew Brindle/Miriam Andrews Lademan
Every child has at one time or other wished he was small enough to hide somewhere unobserved. The writers of this story bring a little caterpillar into a church by way of a lady's purse and appeal to child readers by allowing the little caterpillar to be as curious as they are. The caterpillar goes from being scared, to being curious, to being in awe. This hungry little caterpillar desires the love and truth that only God can give us. Readers see the holy sacrifice of the Mass through the interesting, new perspective of the caterpillar.

Pascual and the Kitchen Angels
Written and Illustrated by Tomie dePaola
Have you ever heard the story of St. Paschal? Most people haven't, but little cooks and big cooks alike will delight in discovering the patron saint of cooks and the domestic kitchen. St. Paschal was a simple Franciscan friar whose only goal in life was to feed and help people in need. Instead, he was put in charge of the Franciscan monastery kitchen and meals. In this beautifully illustrated picture book, author-illustrator Tomie dePaola focuses on the legend of the kitchen angels who supposedly came to Paschal's rescue in the kitchen.

Lovely Lady Dressed in Blue and the Knights of Our Lady
Written and Illustrated by Joan Andrews Bell/ Susan Andrews Brindle/ Miriam Andrews Lademan
The story begins with Aunt Miriam taking the children for a picnic in the woods. The setting is so much like Robin Hood's Sherwood Forest that the children forget themselves and actually become medieval knights. But the children have an inner yearning to be part of something stronger and more lasting than they are. So when they voice their wishes to be good Christian knights like the Crusaders, Aunt Miriam gives them their appointments. They are to be soldiers for Christ, like St. Dominic was, and fight the good fight using the rosary as their weapon. This beautiful, inspiring, uplifting reading is great for children ages 1 to 100 and perfect for Confirmation candidates and for celebrating any Marian feast.

Karol from Poland
Written by M. Leonora Wilson/ Illustrated by Carla Koch
This beautiful picture book introduces children to the life of the Great Pope John Paul II. The book includes his youth in Poland, his school years, and the time until he became Pope. Come meet the man we know today as Pope John Paul II the Great.

The Princess and the Kiss
Written by Jennie Bishop/ Illustrated by Preston McDaniels

A lesson in purity is the best way to describe this story in which a princess is given the gift of a kiss on the day she is born. It is hers to keep or give to someone else and she realizes how precious it is. The kiss is kept safe in the castle tower until the princess is of age to marry. She meets numerous suitors, but she realizes that none of them can give her the one thing that she can in turn give them. Then a humble farmer comes to the princess and offers his gift. You can guess the rest but your daughters in particular will enjoy this lovely story.

The Twelve Apostles
Written and Illustrated by Marianna Mayer

This book serves as an excellent introduction to the 12 close friends of Jesus. Who were they? Where were they from? What did they do after the passion, death and resurrection of Christ? How can you recognize them in religious artwork? All of your kids will enjoy this very interesting, scholarly work.

The Blackbird's Nest: A Tale of St. Kevin of Ireland
Written by Jenny Schroedel/ Illustrated by Doug Montross

While little is known of St. Kevin of Ireland, this little tale shares a legend that has evolved around St. Kevin. I encourage parents who have a child with autism, Asperger Syndrome, or another behavioral label such as ADD /ADHD to read this book to your child. Other parents are encouraged to read this book as well and discuss with their child someone they know who might have behavioral problems. We need to remember that "special needs" children are blessed by God and have the potential to become great saints.

Across a Dark and Wild Sea
Written and Illustrated by Don Brown

This book about St. Columcille is sure to have the reader rethinking the way he looks at books and literature in our modern day world. St. Columcille's work helped to light the candle of literacy and truth for all people. Some Catholics might not be impressed with the way St. Finnian is depicted in this story but, until an illustrated book is written about St. Finnian, we must ask our children to think charitably of him, do some research concerning him, and be glad that our child is being introduced to such a little known historical figure. Please note that this book serves a very important purpose in this study by showing us how much influence one person can have in the world of knowledge and education. It also serves to instill a sense of appreciation for the monks whose preservation efforts gave us the wealth of literature and learning we enjoy today.

The Legend of Saint Christopher
Written by Margaret Hodges/ Illustrated by Richard Jesse Watson
Christopher: The Holy Giant
Written and Illustrated by Tomie dePaola

Sadly, we seldom hear about dear St. Christopher any more. Introduce your child to him using these two delightful stories. He will soon grow to love the story of this saint who has carried many travelers upon his shoulders.

A Peek into My Church
Written by Wendy Goody & Veronica Kelly/ Illustrated by Ginny Pruitt
This book is the most colorful, detailed book on church participation ever written. Its tone is cheerful without being trite. A child will feel right at home in the pages of this book and will feel inspired to observe more closely the traditional items inside his own church.

Sister Anne's Hands
Written by Marybeth Lorbiecki/ Illustrated by K. Wendy Popp
In this masterfully told and beautifully illustrated story, a new teacher comes to Anna's school. It is the 1960s and the children at first are not sure what to make of this new teacher. She is African American and a nun. But her reformed way of teaching draws the children to her. She's clever, funny, and wonderful. Everyone is getting along famously until . . . a paper airplane swoops down and lands near Sister Anne. The note found on the paper airplane is menacing and hateful. Sister Anne takes it upon herself to teach a new lesson at the school—a lesson to teach the children the "colors of hatred." Sister Anne teaches the children that when they close doors, they risk closing the door on God.

Juanita and Our Lady of the Angels
Written and Illustrated by Elizabeth Loch
Get ready for a trip to Costa Rica and a trip to a Marian shrine that many Catholics are not familiar with. This is a true story of the mysterious rock doll that a girl named Juanita finds on a hill. She takes the doll back to her hut and hides it, but the next morning, it has vanished. She finds it again in the same spot on the hill and again vanishes after she has taken it home. She finally asks a priest to help her solve the mystery. The priest notices the doll's image is that of a mother holding her infant son. What happens when the priests locks the doll in the tabernacle? Read this book and you will discover the miracle and unveil the shrine that is dedicated to our Blessed Mother.

Brother Bartholomew and the Apple Grove
Written by Jan Cheripko/ Illustrated by Kestutis Kasparavicius
This book is not about Saint Bartholomew but rather a brother monk who is his namesake. Brother Bartholomew is tending the apple grove at the monastery when a new brother monk, Brother Stephen, arrives. He finds fault with everything Brother Bartholomew does. Brother Stephen begins to dwell on what a success the apple grove would be if only he were in charge of it. With the earthly passing of old Brother Bartholomew, the new monk is given the apple grove to tend. He begins with big hopes and bright ideas, only to find that "Pride cometh before a fall."

Some readers have suggested that the book hints at reincarnation in the end: Has Brother Bartholomew come back as a deer? However, the author intends only that the look in the deer's eyes reminds Brother Stephen of the look in Brother Bartholomew's eyes— the look of sorrowful accusation. The real meditation in this book is for the reader to ask himself what Brother Stephen asked himself: "Where is your heart? What is your treasure?" And the real message is to realize: "God provides. He always does."

Mother Teresa
Written and Illustrated by Demi

With respect and awe for this saintly servant of God, Demi offers a very detailed account of Mother Teresa's life and work. The author includes many of Mother Teresa's own words and pictures while telling her story. Children will find a very accessible saint within the pages of this book.

Peter Claver, Patron Saint of Slaves
Written by Julia Durango/ Illustrated by Rebecca Garcia-Franco

For years I knew next to nothing about this saint—only that a small nearby mission church was named under his patronage. Reading this book gave me a quick, gentle summary of St. Peter Claver's mission and his undying determination to serve as shepherd and witness to God's people. This is a lovely telling of his story serving the slaves in Colombia, South America.

The Tale of Three Trees
Retold by Angela Elwell Hunt / Illustrated by Tim Jonke

Three trees stand in a forest and they all have grand visions of becoming something magestic: a beautiful treasure chest, a mighty sailing ship, and the tallest tree in the forest so that people might look to heaven and think of God. Then one fateful day they are all chopped down to become what they least expected. This book's storyline is a spiritual treasure in itself, but when you consider the beautiful artwork as well, you'll agree that The Tale of Three Trees demands a place on every Christian family's bookshelf.

St. Jerome and the Lion
Retold by Margaret Hodges/ Illustrated by Barry Moser

Have you ever seen a picture of a saint with a lion at his side? Chances are you saw St. Jerome in his study full of books; after all, he is the patron saint of librarians. If you are interested in the story of how a lion came to occupy the library with St. Jerome, read this impressively illustrated book.

Angel in the Waters
Written by Regina Doman/ Illustrated by Ben Hatke

This absolutely luscious book by Regina Doman was inspired by something told to her by a small child. It has become a pro-life treasure and makes a perfect gift for any new mother. Children will be intrigued to find themselves inside the mysterious confines of a mother with a small angel's voice guiding them into the larger real world. They will realize that God is watching out for us in many different ways—sometimes very small ways. Surely, those who read this book will be left with a remembrance of a little voice that has guided them throughout their lives.

My Guardian Dear
Written and Illustrated by Miriam Lademan & Susan Brindle

Another lovely colorful illustrated book by the Andrews sisters, My Guardian Angel, shows us how every person has an angelic being assigned to accompany him—and only him—throughout life. Your child will enjoy meeting Angela's angel Gloriel and traveling with him to meet saints who were spiritually close to their guardian angels.

The Good Man of Assisi
Written by Mary Joslin/ Illustrated by Alison Wisenfeld
Growing up, Francis had it all. He had money, friends, clothes, and good food. He was enjoying his life when suddenly, in the midst of everything, Francis remembered God. He heard God tell him to, "Come, follow me." Francis gave up everything to follow Christ. A peace-maker and lover of nature, he helped others and was a friend to all of God's creations, even birds, snakes, and wolves. This book will show children how to strive to live a saintly life.

A Saint and His Lion
Written by Elaine Murray Stone/ Illustrated by Cecile Sharratt
Don't let the title of this book fool you! There is much more to this story than a boy and a lion. A Saint and His Lion tells you about a real saint who overcame many adversities to spread the word and love of Christ across his country of Ethiopia. Even a broken leg and a lion could not deter him. In the manner of St. Francis of Assisi, St. Tekla turned bad things into greater goods, all for God's kingdom.

Father Phillip Tells a Ghost Story, A Story of Divine Mercy
Written and Illustrated by Miriam Andrews Lademan/ Susan Andrews Brindle
Some of us enjoy a good ghost story. Since ghosts (or spirits) do exist, this book is an interesting way to refute the secular view of ghosts and to expose children to the Catholic teachings on spiritual beings. Fr. Phillip comes to watch the children while their parents go out. Fr. Phillip entertains them with some true ghost stories. He relates the truth of Purgatory and tells about the suffering souls who need our prayers. This story is a real eye-opener for Catholic families who are struggling with how to merge their faith and the secular Halloween festivities into one family tradition.

I Sing a Song of the Saints of God
Written by Lesbia Scott/ Illustrated by Judith Gwyn Brown
This book brings to life a simple hymn written in 1920 by Lesbia Scott for her own children. This hymn was circulated and inevitably put to music (the music score is found at the back of the book). The pictures by Judith Gwyn Brown guide the parent and child through the hymn. They portray modern-day children acting out a play of the saints who have "gone before them marked with the sign of faith." Young readers will see how we are all "called to be saints" and how we can be saints just like those who lived in "ages past." Indeed, your child will see that saints are all around us every day—in the most ordinary places.

The Spirit of Tio Fernando
Written by Janice Levy/ Illustrated by Morella Fuenmayor
This book by Janice Levy narrates an old Catholic Hispanic tradition of setting up an altar in the home and visiting the cemetery on the Feast of All Souls Day. While not every parent will agree to observe the Day of the Dead on All Souls Day, it is very much in

keeping with the Catholic calendar and should be read together with Fr. Phillip Tells a Ghost Story. Some Catholics will see the resemblance between this feast day and the feast day of St. Joseph, when families create St. Joseph Altars.

Brother Joseph, The Painter of Icons
Written by Fr. Augustine DeNoble, O.S.B./ Illustrated by Judith Brown

Have you ever wondered why saints drawn in icons look so awkward or out of balance? Have you ever wondered what those other symbols on an icon mean? This book is the perfect book to begin your study of icon art, answering your questions and showing how icons are a form of prayer.

Saint Francis and the Christmas Donkey
Written and Illustrated by Robert Byrd

This lovely find for any family captures the same pleasure children find in stories and pictures of Noah's Ark. There are animals galore! The donkey in this story is a sad creature who has caused his own tale of woe but, by story's end, has made amends for his prideful and vain behavior and been redeemed by Christ. Do not overlook the Author's Note at the end, even if your children don't want to sit and listen. You will find a lot of interesting information there about the story and St. Francis.

The Clown of God
Written and Illustrated by Tomie dePaola

In this poignant story, poor Giovanni represents each one of us. We really have nothing to offer Christ but our talents and our love. Each of us is but a little ball, a play thing, in His hands. He can do with us what He wills. Like Giovanni, sometimes our cares in the world make us lose sight of our real purpose in life. Giovanni teaches us that we should seek to make those around us happy because, by doing so, we make Christ happy—and Christ is our ultimate audience.

The Miracle of Saint Nicholas
Written by Gloria Whelan/ Illustrated by Judith Brown

Although her village church stands deserted and discarded in Soviet Russia, Alexi's babushka has dreams of its becoming once again the church from her childhood, lit with candles and full of family and friends. Alexi sets out to make his babushka's dream come true. His work in cleaning the church motivates the other villagers to reveal secrets that they have kept hidden for many, many years. And the shoemaker has the biggest secret of all. This story is a delightful read.

The Lady of Guadalupe
Written and Illustrated by Tomie dePaola

There is more to the story of Our Lady of Guadalupe than just the apparition of the Blessed Mother. We cannot forget Juan Diego, whose feast day is December 9. DePaola's rendering of the story highlights Juan Diego's perspective. The illustrations in the book are filled with images of Catholic home life, and the images of the Lady of Guadalupe are worthy of Mary's beauty. All who read this story will treasure its historical vision of Guadalupe.

The Legend of the Poinsettia
Written and Illustrated by Tomie dePaola

In this beautiful holiday story, Lucida is proud that her mother has been asked to help make a new blanket for baby Jesus in the la Navidad Christmas play. Her joy is short-lived when her mother becomes sick and cannot finish the blanket. Lucida tries to finish it but her attempts meet with failure. Heartbroken, she must go to the la Navidad play with nothing but a patch of tall green weeds—her only offering to the baby Jesus. The weeds are miraculously transformed, however, and the poinsettia blooms.

The Donkey's Dream
Written and Illustrated by Barbara Helen Berger

Using simple and refined, yet beautifully profound prose, the author gives careful consideration to the various symbols of Mary found throughout the history of the Church. She even gives the reader clues to finding the les yeux de Marie (Mary's eyes) which are sprinkled throughout the book. Its message is a wonderful one to hear on any feast day that honors our Blessed Mother.

The Crippled Lamb
Written by Max Lucado/ Illustrated by Liz Bonahm

Who can deny the appeal of a lamb, especially a crippled lamb, who befriends a wise old cow named Abigail. When Josh, the crippled lamb, is unable to follow the other farm animals on to greener pastures due to his crippled leg, he is forced to stay behind with Abigail and sleep in the barn. But what a wondrous night to sleep in the old barn—the same wondrous night when a couple finds shelter in the old barn and Josh finds his rightful place beside a newborn babe. You and your children will enjoy this sweet holiday story.

Art Interpretation

A special piece of artwork was created for this book for each month of the year. Each drawing contains clues to the events of the liturgical year that take place in that month. Some are straightforward representations, some are symbolic. See if your child can find the following things in each of the drawings.

January

Holy Family
Epiphany
St. Agnes

February

Chair of St. Peter
Our Lady of Lourdes
St. Blaise
St. Valentine

March

Annunciation
St. Gregory the Great
St. Thomas Aquinas
St. Patrick

Lent

Temptation in the Desert
April
Holy Thursday
Good Friday
Easter Sunday
Opening the Gates of Heaven
St. Mark

May

Ascension
Our Lady's Month
St. Joseph the Worker

June

Pentecost
Saints Peter and Paul
Feast of the Sacred Heart of Jesus
Nativity of John the Baptist

July

Weddings
Feast of the Precious Blood of Jesus

August

Transfiguration
Assumption

September

Triumph of the Cross
St. Michael
Seven Sorrows of Mary

October

Christ the King
St. Raphael
Guardian Angels

November

Holy Souls
All Saints

December

Advent
St. Nicholas
Immaculate Conception
Christmas
Holy Innocents

January

Sean Fitzpatrick

Mary, Mother of Jesus

Written by Mary Joslin/ Illustrated by Alison Wisenfeld
Illustrations copyright © 1999 Alison Wisenfield. Illustrations taken
from *Mary, Mother of Jesus* by Mary Joslin, published by Lion Hudson plc and
Loyola,1999.

Mary, The Mother of Jesus

Written and Illustrated by Tomie dePaola

FEAST DAY: JANUARY 1, MARY THE MOTHER OF GOD

Discussion Questions

In Tomie dePaola's book:
1. How long did Jesus' ministry last?
2. Whom did Jesus promise He would send to help His mother and His friends?
3. What did the Holy Spirit sound like?
4. What symbols usually represent the Holy Spirit?
5. How was Mary's death different from that of other people?

In Mary Joslin/Alison Wisenfeld's book:
1. What are the yellow circles behind the heads of Mary, Joseph, and Jesus?
2. At the end of the book, Mary is looking away from the crowd. To whom is she speaking?
3. Why is St. John portrayed in this book?

Compare/Contrast

1. Which book do you think has more information in it?
2. Which book's art work do you prefer or like better?

From Both Books
1. Why do you think Mary willingly agreed to become the mother of Christ?
2. What happened when Mary and Joseph presented the infant Jesus in the temple?
3. After Jesus had been lost for three days and then found in the temple, what did he say to Mary and Joseph that they did not understand? What do you think he meant by that?
4. What was Jesus' first miracle?
5. Who asked Him to perform it?

Copywork

My soul magnifies the Lord. He that is mighty has done great things to me and Holy is His name.
—Mary at the Visitation
Luke 1: 46, 49

Little children, let us love one another, not just in what we say but also in what we do. Let us love one another, because love is from God.
— from *Mary, Mother of Jesus* by Alison Joslin

Parent's Help Page
Mary, Mother of Jesus and Mary, The Mother of Jesus

Discussion Answers

In Tomie dePaola's book:
1. 3 years
2. The Holy Spirit

3. A strong wind
4. A dove or a flame of fire
5. She rose into Heaven body and soul.

In Mary Joslin/Alison Wisenfeld's book:
1. Halos. Artists often use this symbol to show that the person was holy.
2. St. John
3. He was a close friend of Jesus who took care of Mary after Jesus died.

Compare/Contrast

1. Answers will vary. Ask the child to explain his answer.
2. Answers will vary. Ask the child to explain his answer.

From Both Books
1. She wanted to do God's will in all things.
2. A holy man named Simeon told Mary that her son would bring joy and salvation to the world. He prophesized that Jesus would be rejected by men and a sword would pierce Mary's motherly heart.
3. "Didn't you know I was in my Father's House?"
4. Changing water into wine at the wedding in Cana
5. His mother.

Enrichment Activities

Mary is sometimes depicted as Our Lady of Sorrows, with seven swords piercing her heart. These seven swords symbolize the seven chief sorrows that Our Lady suffered during her life. Another name for Mary is Our Lady of Seven Dolors, or Seven Sorrows.

Simeon gives the prophecy that Mary's heart will be pierced by a sword.
Mary and Joseph flee with Baby Jesus into Egypt.
The Child Jesus is lost for three days.
Mary meets Jesus on the road to Calvary.
Jesus is crucified and dies.
Jesus is taken down from the cross.
Jesus is laid in the tomb.

(See Appendix B and C for more activity suggestions.)

by Hans Christian Andersen  illustrated by Rachel Isadora

The Little Match Girl

Written by Hans Christian Andersen/ Illustrated by Rachel Isadora
Published by Penguin Group, 1987.

Cover reprinted by permission of the publisher.

TWELVE DAYS OF CHRISTMAS

Vocabulary

copper	sputter	merchant	transparent
perish	vanish	distinctly	halo
misery			

Discussion Questions

1. Why is the little girl "wandering in the dark cold streets"?
2. Is she dressed appropriately? Why not?
3. Why does she feel safer in the cold street corner than she does at home?
4. Do you think there are children who live in the streets today?
5. What can we do to help them?
6. Which Corporal Acts of Mercy do we perform when we help the poor?
7. Why did the little girl light the matches?
8. What did she see?
9. Where did the little girl go at the end of the book?

Copywork

When a star falls, a soul is going up to God.

—from *The Little Match Girl* by Hans Christian Anderson,

Parent's Help Page

The Little Match Girl

Discussion Answers

1. The little girl is selling matches.
2. No, she is not dressed appropriately. She is dressed in rags and has no bonnet or shoes.
3. She feels safer on the street because she has not sold any matches and her father will beat her if she goes home with no money. Her house is cold because the wind blows through the cracks.
4. Yes.
5. Listen carefully to your child's reply; then reference the Corporal Works of Mercy found below.
6. See below.
7. She lit the matches to warm herself.
8. First match — a stove with a warm fire
   Second match — a festive table with a roast goose that
       waddled across the floor
   Third match — a Christmas tree
   Fourth match — her grandmother
9. At the end, the little girl is taken to Heaven to be with her Grandmother and God.

Enrichment Activity

Study and learn the Corporal Works of Mercy. Have your child write each work on an index card, and then find a picture from a magazine that illustrates the work. Have him cut out the picture and glue it on the opposite side of the appropriate index card. Store these cards in your Liturgical Year Notebook.

> Feed the hungry.
> Give drink to the thirsty.
> Clothe the naked.
> Visit the imprisoned.
> Shelter the homeless.
> Visit the sick.
> Bury the dead.

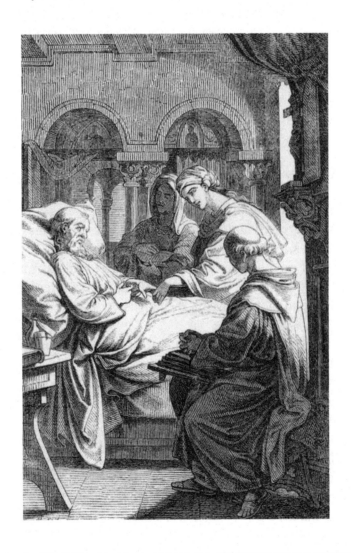

The Last Straw

Written by Fredrick H. Thury/ Illustrated by Vlasta van Kampen
Published by Charlesbridge Publishing, 1998.
Cover reprinted by permission of the publisher.

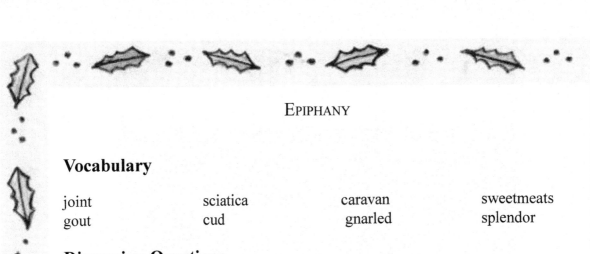

Vocabulary

joint   sciatica   caravan   sweetmeats
gout   cud   gnarled   splendor

Discussion Questions

1. What type of events did Hoshmakaka like to go to?
2. Why did Hoshmakaka brag about himself to the other camels?
3. What did Hoshmakaka tell his camel friends?
4. Why did others ask Hoshmakaka to carry their gifts to the new baby king?
5. What did Hoshmakaka moan would bring him to his ruin?
6. What was his "fruit of the vine"?
7. What was the last gift that made Hoshmakaka's legs wobble, his back feel like it was breaking, and caused him to fall?
8. What disappeared at the touch of the baby's hand?
9. Why did his pain disappear?
10. What quote do we often use today that reminds us of this story? What does it mean?

Copywork

As the branch cannot bear fruit of itself unless it remain on the vine, so neither can you unless you abide in Me. I Am the vine, you are the branches. He who abides in Me, and I in him, he bears much fruit; for without Me, you can do nothing.
— John 15:4-5

Come unto me, all you who labor and are burdened, and I will give you rest. Take my yoke upon you, and learn from me; for I am meek and humble of heart; and you shall find rest for your souls. For my yoke is easy, and my burden light.
— Matthew 11: 28-30

Parent's Help Page
The Last Straw

Observation

1. List the gifts Hoshmakaka ended up carrying to Bethlehem:

   Wise men—frankincense, myrrh, gold
   Herd of mountain goats—milk
   Family of millers—ground corn
   Two ladies—fine silks
   An old man—two rare birds in silver cages
   Some merchants—pillars of oak from Lebanon
   Group of bakers —sweetmeats and pastries
   People—jars of honey, baskets of money, jewels, beads, large rolls of leather, and 20 gallons of wine

2. Compare the illustrations of Hoshmakaka on the opening pages to the one of him kneeling in front of the nativity. See how many of the gifts you can find on Hoshmakaka.

Discussion Answers

1. Hoshmakaka liked to go to water-drinking competitions and cud-chewing conventions.
2. Hoshmakaka bragged about himself to the other camels because they all looked up to him, thinking him wise and special.
3. Hoshmakaka told his camel friends that he was "as strong as ten horses."
4. Others asked Hoshmakaka to carry their gifts because they thought he was strong.
5. Hoshmakaka said that the "this fruit of the vine" would bring him to ruin.
6. Hoshmakaka's "fruit of the vine" was the work he was doing for the newborn king.
7. A little boy's piece of straw for the newborn king's bed.
8. Hoshmakaka's pain seemed to disappear. *"He could no longer feel his burden."*
9. His pain disappeared because Jesus has said *"Come unto me, all ye that labor and are heavy laden, and I will give you rest."*
10. People often use this familiar expression: "The straw that broke the camel's back." This quote refers to any task that we feel will bring us to our knees, usually after we have endured much toil already.

A Gift of Gracias
Written by Julia Alvarez / Illustrated by Beatriz Vidal

FEAST DAY: JANUARY 21, OUR LADY OF HIGH GRACE
(Nuestra Senora de la Altagracia)

Vocabulary

prosper   yield

Discussion Questions

1. What was Maria's Papa—and other farmers—trying to grow?
2. What gift did Maria ask her Papa for?
3. What does *"gracias"* and *"Muchas gracias"* mean in English?
4. What does *Nuestra Senora de la Altagracia* mean?
5. Who is *Nuestra Senora de la Altagracia*?
6. Did anyone at the market have a picture of *Nuestra Senora de la Altagracia*?
7. What did Quisqueya gather in the blanket that had covered his shoulders?
8. How did Maria and her parents finish gathering the oranges at night?
9. Why was Maria's family so thankful at the end of the story?

Copywork

Maria could not think of anything she wanted more
than to see the beautiful lady, night and day. To say
gracias and feel that sweetness in her heart again.
— from *Gift of Gracias* by Julia Alvarez

Parent's Help Page
A Gift of Gracias

Observation

Notice the color scheme that the illustrator chose for this story. See if you can
describe the colors. For example, are they vibrant, warm, cool, comforting?
Notice all the different shades of green that the artist used. How does the green
make you feel when you see the paintings? Look at the paintings of the inside of
the house. What colors did the artist chose there? What feelings do those colors
evoke? If you were to paint a picture of your house, what colors would bring out
the feelings you have for your home.

Discussion Answers

1. They were trying to grow olives like they had in Spain.
2. Maria asked that her father come back safely.
3. *"Gracias"* means "Thank you" and *"Muchas gracias"* means "Many thanks."
4. *Nuestra Senora de la Altagracia* means Our Lady of Thanks.
5. *Nuestra Senora de la Altagracia* is our Blessed Mother, Mary.
6. No one had a picture of *Nuestra Senora de la Altagracia*.
7. Quisqueya gathered the stars falling from the sky.

8. They gathered the oranges by the light of the stars on the blanket.
9. Maria's family was able to keep their farm.

Enrichment Activities

1. Locate Spain on a map or globe. Locate the Dominican Republic on a map or globe. Label them on your maps. You may use the maps provided in the Appendix.
2. Read the last two sentences on the page where Maria, her Papa, and Quisqueya are at the table. Eat an orange while you read the sentences.

> *"It smelled sharp and fresh, like tickling inside her nose. It tasted like a sweet sunrise, tingling inside her mouth."*

Now you write in your own words how your orange tasted and smelled.
3. Read "About the Story" at the back of book. Since the feast day of the Dominican Republic's little *"virgencita"*—*Nuestra Senora de la Altagracia*—is in January, start now to keep track of all Marian Apparitions this year. Collect prayer cards of the various Marian apparitions and keep them in a plastic page protector inside your Liturgical Year Notebook. (See Appendix A for a list of Marian Feast Days.) As you collect and study the holy cards, observe differences and similarities. In which ones does the ethnic flavor of the feast day or apparition shine through? Are there any initials or symbols in the picture? What do they mean?
4. Make a collage of all the things that you are thankful for.

February

Sean Fitzpatrick

The Most Beautiful Thing
in the World

La Plus Belle Chose Sur la Terre

La Cosa más Bella del Mundo

Adapted from a story by
Rev. Gerald T. Brennan

Illustrated by: Susan Andrews Brindle   Ann Gershona Brindle   Margaret Mary Brindle

The Most Beautiful Thing in the World

Adapted from Story by Rev. Gerald T. Brennan/ Illustrated by Susan
Andrews Brindle, Ann Gershona Brindle, Margaret Mary Brindle

Published by Precious Life Books, Inc, 2004.

Cover reprinted by permission of the publisher.

SACRAMENT OF CONFESSION

Vocabulary

aroma   precious   stoop   melodies
celebration   trumpets   harmonious

Discussion

1. What did the angels tell the youngest angel to go and do?
2. What was the first beautiful thing the youngest angel found on earth?
3. Was the rose the most beautiful thing?
4. What other beautiful things did he find?
5. Where any of these things the most beautiful?
6. Why was the little girl in church crying?
7. What did the little angel pick up and take to heaven?
8. What is the most beautiful thing in the world?

Copywork

> Oh my God, I am heartily sorry for having offended
> Thee, and I detest all my sins because of Thy
> just punishment; but most of all, because I have
> offended, Thee, my God, Who art all good and
> deserving of all my love. I firmly resolve, with the
> help of Thy grace, to sin no more and to avoid the
> near occasion of sin. Amen.
>   — traditional Act of Contrition

Parent's Help Page
The Most Beautiful Thing in the World

Observation and Enrichment Activity

Join your child in a walk outside today. Observe all the gifts of beauty God has given us. Bring a camera and take snapshots of various things. Try to find the things mentioned in the book: birds, butterflies, puppies, kittens, etc. Lastly, take a picture of your child. After the pictures are developed, place them on a sheet of paper, and then write the words "Beautiful Things God has Made" at the top. On the back of this sheet, or on another sheet of paper, write at the top "The Most Beautiful Thing in the World," and place the picture of your child under the heading. Have him rewrite the copywork under his picture. Place this in your Liturgical Year Notebook.

Discussion Answers

1. The angels told the youngest angel to go to earth and find the most beautiful thing in the world.
2. He found a big, bright, delicious red rose.
3. No.
4. He found rivers, mountains, pretty birds, butterflies, puppies, ponies, kittens, and a little baby.
5. No.
6. The little girl was thinking of her sins and how they hurt Jesus. She was crying because she was sorry for her sins.
7. The little angel picked up the girl's teardrop.
8. The most beautiful thing in the world is a truly repentant soul, a soul that loves God above all else. Our love is the only thing we can give to Our Lord.

Brigid's Cloak

Written by Bryce Milligan/ Illustrated by Helen Cann
Published by Eerdmans, 2005.
Cover reprinted by permission of the publisher.

FEAST DAY: FEBRUARY 1, ST. BRIGID OF IRELAND

Vocabulary

thatch   dense   tattered   ladling   generosity

Discussion Questions

1. Find Ireland on a globe or map and then label it on your map.
2. What did Druids worship?

3. Whom do Christians worship, both then and today?
4. What familiar religious scene did Brigid become a part of?
5. To whom did Brigid give her cloak?
6. Can you think of any other saints who were privileged to hold the Baby Jesus?
7. When Brigid's mother found her in the stable what had happened to her blue cloak?

Copywork

Blessed are you among all women, and blessed is your holy child.

—Brigid's words to Mary in *Brigid's Cloak.*

Parent's Help Page
Brigid's Cloak

Discussion Answers
1. Help child locate Ireland on globe or map and label it on world map.
2. Druids worshiped nature and other false gods.
3. Christians worship the one true God.
4. She became part of the Nativity scene
5. Brigid gave her cloak to Mary.
6. Your child may think of St. Anthony or St. Christopher.
7. Brigid's cloak had changed and looked new again with dozens of stars upon it.

Enrichment Activity

1. Find a scrap of blue cloth or felt at least 8½ × 11 inches. Let your child stick gold or silver star stickers all over the outside front flap. Then glue a holy card of St. Brigid of Ireland inside the folded piece of blue cloth or felt.
2. Glue a holy card to a nice piece of blue paper. Under the holy card print the words:

    May God keep you safe under St. Brigid's cloak.
    Fa bhrat Bhrighde

The child may decorate the paper with stars if desired. This can be given as a gift or placed in the Liturgical Year Notebook. (Be sure to read the Historical Note at the back of the book for an explanation of this quote.)

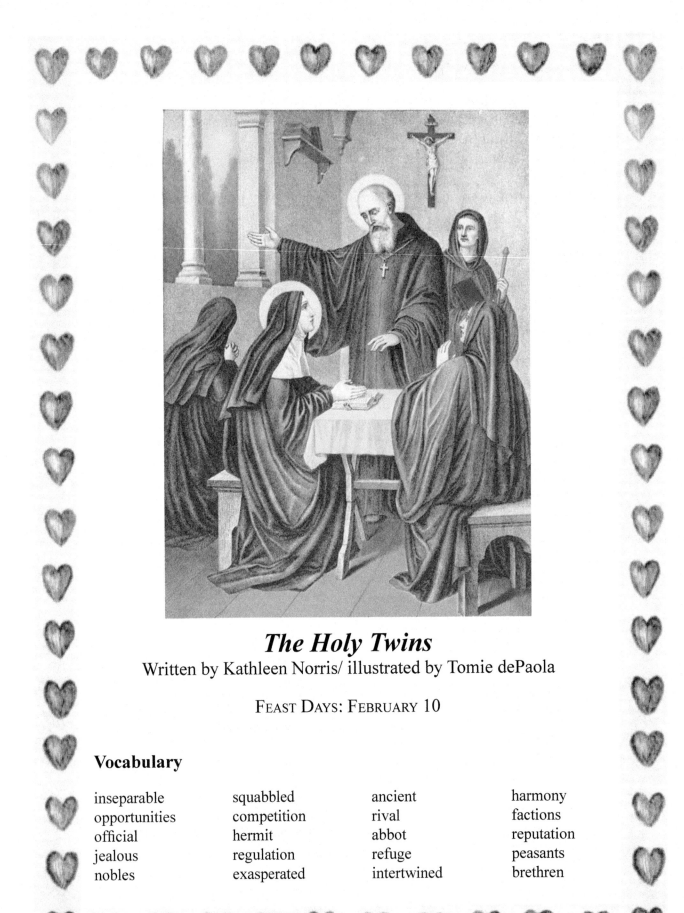

The Holy Twins
Written by Kathleen Norris/ illustrated by Tomie dePaola

FEAST DAYS: FEBRUARY 10

Vocabulary

inseparable	squabbled	ancient	harmony
opportunities	competition	rival	factions
official	hermit	abbot	reputation
jealous	regulation	refuge	peasants
nobles	exasperated	intertwined	brethren

Discussion Questions

1. Find the town of Nursia in northern Italy and label it on your map.
2. What day of the year is the feast day of St. Benedict and St. Scholastica?
3. Why did others try to poison St. Benedict?
4. Where did St. Scholastica learn all the things her brother had learned from his travels? Why did she find this amusing?
5. Go back to the front of the book where the author and illustrator have their dedications. On the right hand side of the spread is a circular symbol with the initials "C. S. P." and "B." in it. Look at the bottom of the dedications on the lefthand side to find out what the letters stand for. What does the circular symbol is the symbol?

Copywork

One must listen to others with the 'ear of the heart.
—Scholastica's advice to her brother Benedict in
The Holy Twins by Kathleen Norris

Parent's Help Page

The Holy Twins

Observation

1. Look for pictures of Saint Benedict and Saint Scholastica on each page of the book. Illustrator Tomie dePaola took special care to draw these two saints on each page.
2. Make a list of religious images found in book.

Discussion Answers

1. Help child locate Nursia, Italy, on globe or map and then label it on a world map.
2. St. Scholastica's feast day is on February 10.
   St. Benedict's feast day is on July 11.
3. They were jealous of St. Benedict and wanted to get rid of him.
4. ". . . she had learned by trial and error in her own monastery." She found this amusing because as she says, *"Isn't it funny, Brother, that you had to travel all over Italy to learn some of the things I discovered by staying in one place!"*
5. The letters "C. S. P." and "B." stand for *Crux Sancti Patris Benedicti*, or Cross of the Holy Father Benedict. The symbol is the Cross of St. Benedict.

Enrichment Activities

St. Scholastica

1. St. Scholastica is traditionally represented in paintings carrying a crosier and a crucifix. She is also portrayed with a dove, in memory of the miracle depicted in this story (she prayed for a storm to keep her brother with her since she knew she was close to dying and would not see him again). Sometimes the dove is on her shoulder; sometimes it is in her hand or sitting next to her; and sometimes it is coming out of her mouth. Visit these web addresses to view paintings of St. Scholastica.

   http://www.artcyclopedia.com/artists/detail/Detail_restout_jean.html?noframe
   http://www.magnificat.ca/cal/engl/02-10.htm
   http://www.benedictinemonks.com/bnmonk13.htm

   Ask your child to create a collage of the symbols of St. Scholastica, or combine them in some way in a painting.

2. For younger children, cut out a cross from brown construction paper or plastic foam. Then cut out a picture of a crosier. Glue the crosier to the Cross and write St. Scholastica's name on the back of the cross. Discuss why St. Scholastica would have a crosier as her symbol when usually it is a bishop's symbol. (Keep in mind that she was the abbess of her convent.)

St. Benedict

(Feast day July 11. You may want to save these activities for July and revisit this book then.)

1. Trace the Cross of St. Benedict on a blank sheet of paper. Then color it so that it looks like the one in the book. Place this is your Liturgical Year Notebook.

2. Build a simple "ladder" using popsicle sticks. Make sure there are 12 rungs on your ladder. Glue your ladder on a sheet of construction paper, and write "St. Benedict's Ladder of Humility" at the top of the page. Then, with a pen or marker, label each rung:

   1. Practice Fear and Remembrance of God
   2. Follow the Example of the Savior
   3. Obey God and His Church
   4. Be Patient and Endure
   5. Confess One's Sins
   6. Be Content
   7. Consider Yourself Lower Than Others
   8. Follow the Example of the Saints
   9. Restrain Your Tongue
   10. Be Serious-Minded
   11. Use Few and Gentle Words
   12. Practice Humility of the Heart

Saint Valentine
Retold and Illustrated by Robert Sabuda

FEAST DAY: FEBRUARY 14

Vocabulary

mosaic   emperor   herb   uprising
mandrake   physician   crocus   papyrus

Discussion Questions

1. What was Valentine's trade (or job)?
2. What kinds of things did Valentine keep in his workroom?
3. What did he use to clean wounds?
4. What did Valentine take as payment for his services?
5. Did Valentine have the freedom to go to church like you do? How was he able to worship God?
6. Why did he have to hide? What did the Romans do to Christians?
7. In reality, Valentine was not just a physician. What was he?
8. Why was Valentine thrown into jail?
9. What did he write the first Valentine note on?
10. What was inside the Valentine?
11. What happened to the little girl?

Copywork

If you are upbraided for the name of Christ, blessed
will you be, because the honor, glory and the power
of God and his spirit rest upon you.

— 1Peter 4:14

Parent's Help Page
Saint Valentine

Observation

Thinking about other illustrated books you've read, what is so different about
Robert Subuda's pictures? The illustrator has done his artwork in a mosaic print.
A mosaic is artwork created from small pieces of colored glass or stone. The
pieces of glass or stone are fitted together to make the picture. You see mosaic art
often in churches and cathedrals.

Discussion Answers

1. St. Valentine was a physician.
2. The room had a cabinet full of herbs and powders, animal fat and beeswax,
   wine, milk, and honey.
3. He cleaned wounds with wine and vinegar.
4. People paid Valentine for his services with a jug of wine, baked bread, or
   new sandals.
5. No. Valentine worshipped God only at night in hidden places.
6. Christians had to hide to worship God because the Romans would throw
   them in jail or kill them.
7. Secretly, Valentine was a priest.
8. Valentine was blamed for an uprising in the streets and was thrown into jail
   for it.
9. He wrote on a piece of papyrus.
10. Inside the papyrus was a yellow crocus. (Notice author's note at back of
    book that the crocus is the traditional flower of St. Valentine.)
11. The little girl was cured of her blindness and was able to see the yellow crocus.

Enrichment Activity

Make a mosaic Valentine: Cut out a pink or red construction-paper heart. Cut out
tiny bits of tissue paper of various colors. Glue the tiny colored bits of paper onto
the construction paper heart. Place this in your Liturgical Year Notebook or give it
to a friend.

March

Sean Fitzpatrick

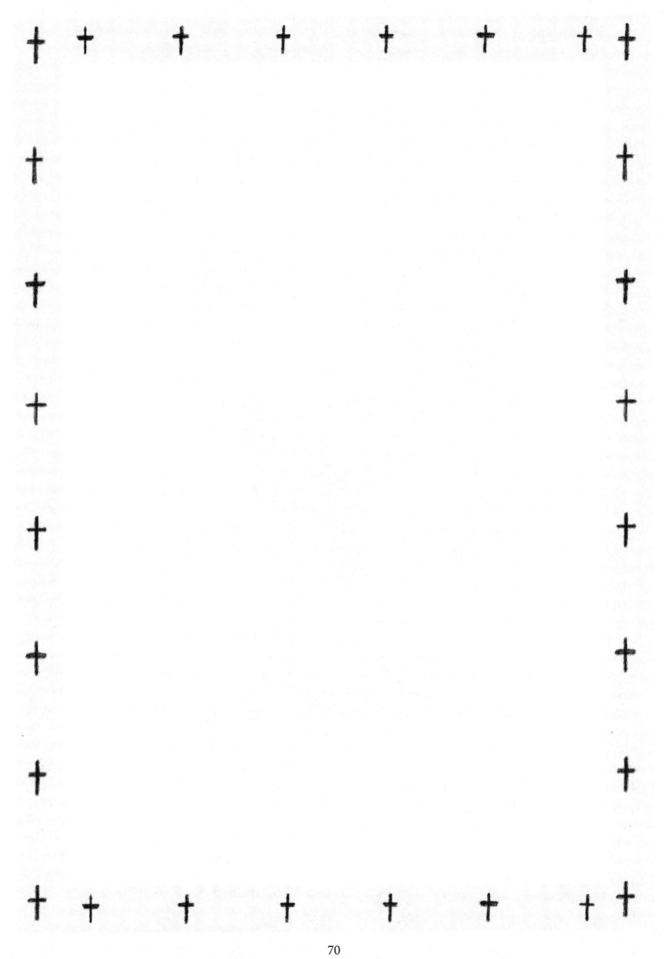

Patrick, Patron Saint of Ireland
Written and Illustrated by Tomie dePaola

FEAST DAY: MARCH 17

Vocabulary

fierce   pagan   deserted   chieftain   chariot

Discussion Questions

1. Find Ireland on a map. Label it.
2. On what day do we honor St. Patrick?
3. What fun tradition do we observe on this day?
4. When the Irishmen raided the British farms and captured the native people, what did Patrick become?
5. What was Patrick's job?
6. Was he happy? What did he do?
7. Name two things God did to help Patrick get back to his family.
8. Why did Patrick leave home again?
9. Why did Patrick feel he had to go back to Ireland?
10. What kinds of people followed Patrick to Ireland?
11. Was Patrick's mission work easy? What were some of the difficulties he faced?
12. What kind of building was converted into Ireland's first church?
13. What symbol is St. Patrick usually associated with?
14. How did St. Patrick use the shamrock to teach the people?

Copywork

"Nothing is impossible for my God," Patrick answered.

—from *St. Patrick, Patron Saint of Ireland* by Tomie DePaola

Parent's Help Page

Patrick, Patron Saint of Ireland

Observation

1. Narrate two of the legends about St. Patrick found at the back of the book.
2. Notice how artist Tomie dePaola draws his pictures in frames, showing various events all on one page. What other illustrated books use frames? (Answer: Comic books)

Discussion Answers

1. Help your child locate Ireland on a map or globe and label it on world map.
2. St. Patrick is honored on March 17.
3. Everyone wears green on that day in honor of St. Patrick and his adopted country of Ireland.
4. Patrick became a slave.
5. Patrick was a shepherd for six years.
6. No, he was not happy; he was lonely. So he prayed to God "over and over and over again."
7. God made the hounds begin to howl until the crew put Patrick on the ship, and He sent them food to eat in the form of a herd of wild pigs so that they would not starve.
8. Patrick left home because he had a dream that told him to return to Ireland.
9. Patrick felt he was being called back to Ireland to tell the people about God and convert them to Christianity.
10. People who followed Patrick to Ireland were priests, bakers, chariot drivers, and others.
11. Patrick's mission work was not easy. It was very hard. The king even tried to kill him and killed his friend instead.
12. Ireland's first church was made from a barn.
13. St. Patrick's symbol is the shamrock.
14. He used the shamrock to teach the people about the *Blessed Trinity*: one God in three Divine Persons: the Father, Son, and Holy Spirit.

Enrichment Activity

Have your child draw or trace a shamrock on paper and label the three leaves: Father, Son, and Holy Spirit. Place this in your Liturgical Year Notebook.

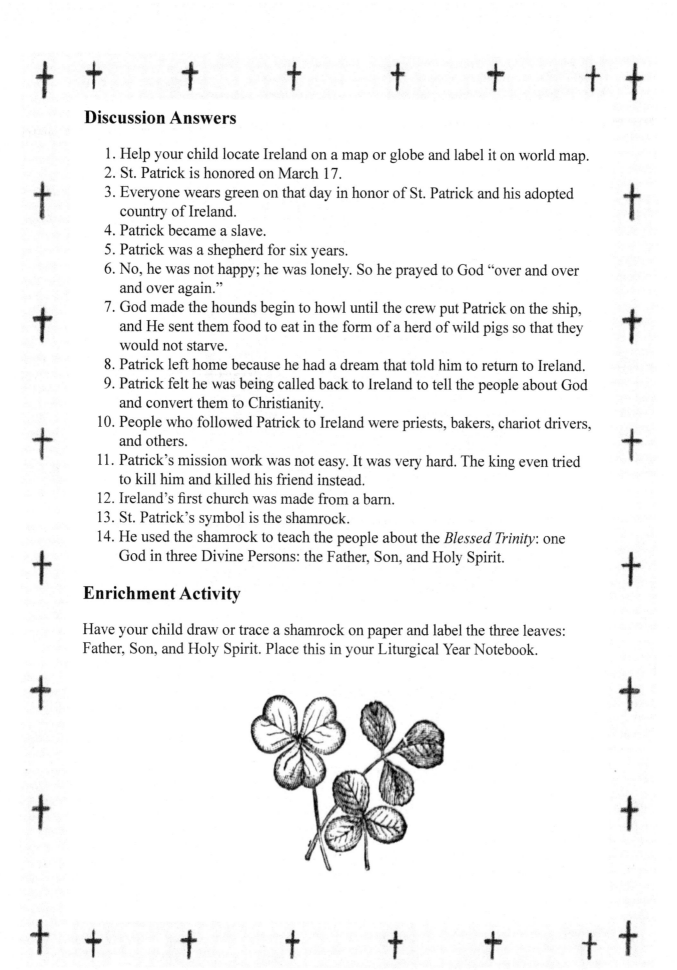

Sean Fitzpatrick

Song of the Swallows
Written and Illustrated by Leo Politi

FEAST DAY: MARCH 19, ST. JOSEPH, SPOUSE OF MARY

Vocabulary

barracks   subdue   enchant   throb   quietude

74

Discussion Questions

1. What does *El Camino Real* mean?
2. Describe what the missions resembled.
3. What was the Spanish name for "swallows"?
4. When did the sparrows come to the mission?
5. Why was Juan careful not to touch the swallow's eggs while counting them?
6. What creature did Julian believe God had given the most freedom and happiness to?
7. Why did Julian think the swallows had come late the following year?

Copywork

Farewell Golondrinas,
For you we will yearn,
May God bless your journey
And guide your return.

—the words of Julian in the story
The Song of the Swallows

Parent's Help Page
Song of the Swallows

Discussion Answers

1. *El Camino Real* means "The Royal Road."
2. The missions resembled little villages.
3. The Spanish name for the swallows is *las golondrinas.*
4. The swallows came to the mission in spring on St. Joseph's Feast Day.
5. Juan did not touch the eggs because he knew the mother and father birds would not like him to do that. It would make them feel that their babies were in danger—and an accident could damage one of the eggs.
6. Julian believed God had given the most freedom and happiness to the birds.
7. Julian believed the swallows were late because they had likely met a storm on the way.

Enrichment Activities

1. A Prayer Garden is a good place to read this story. Does your church have one? It is best to read this story on St. Joseph's Feast Day March 19.
2. Look in a bird guide, encyclopedia, or on the Internet for a picture of a swallow.

3. Find the state of California on a map. Find and trace the California Mission trail on the map.
4. Go on the Internet to locate some of the mission churches founded by Fr. Junipero Serra and his brothers. (Always take care to supervise your children when they are researching on the Web.)
5. Set-up a display table and have a missions/ Indian scavenger hunt. As the items are discovered, place them on the display table.

Suggested items for the Scavenger Hunt:
> A blanket
> Tools
> Pottery
> Corn on cob/ Stalk of wheat
> A basket
> Bricks
> Empty medicine bottles or healing herbs
> Shoe
> Bible
> Jug of wine or bunch of grapes
> Jug of water

6. Sandal Project: Print the list below and cut it out. Trace your child's foot on a piece of brown construction paper. Then have the child cut out the paper foot. Print the list below on a sheet of white paper. Then cut out the list and glue this list to the foot. Place the foot in the Liturgical Notebook.

In addition to protecting the Indians, the priests at the mission taught the Indians to:

> Weave
> make blankets and clothes
> make baskets
> make tools
> tan hides
> make pottery
> grind corn and wheat
> work as blacksmiths
> make bricks
> use herbs as medicine
> read and write
> learn about God
> pray Catholic prayers
> make shoes

farm the gardens
fed them
water irrigation for crops
dig wells
make wine
herd cattle
to be healthy

Other books by Leo Politi

Many of Leo Politi's books are out-of-print. They are worth a good book search.
If you find one, hang onto it.

St. Francis and the Animals
Juanita
The Mission Bell
The Noble Doll
Pedro, the Angel of Olvera Street

Related Stories for Middle School Students

Island of the Blue Dolphins by Scott O'Dell
Pasquala, Story of a California Indian Girl by Gail Faber

Children's Stations of the Cross

Written and Illustrated by Susan Andrews Brindle, Joan Andrews Bell,
Miriam Andrews Lademan
Published by Precious Life Books, Inc, 1997.
Cover reprinted by permission of the publisher.

LENTEN SEASON

Vocabulary

trek	thatch	recessed	crucified	persecuted
conversion	council	creed	chisel	indulgence
votive	reverent	genuflect	offend	redeem
repent	attachment	tomb	contrition	trespass
hallow	resolve	confess		temptation

Discussion Questions

1. What do the Stations of the Cross represent and why do we say them?
2. What does *Via Dolorosa* mean?
3. What is granted to us when we pray the Stations of the Cross?
4. Why did Jesus suffer through the real-life Stations of the Cross?
5. Do you like to follow the Way of the Cross during Lent?
6. Why did Grampa find it so hard to say the Stations of the Cross?
7. What will Jesus do if we pray the Stations of the Cross?
8. Why do are the Stations of the Cross an important devotion in Lent?
9. Why are the Stations said on Fridays?

Copywork

We adore You, O Christ, and we praise You, because by
your holy Cross You have redeemed the world.

—Liturgy of the Way of the Cross

Parent's Help Page
Children's Stations of the Cross

Discussion Answers

1. The Stations of the Cross represent Jesus' walk to Calvary while carrying his cross.
2. It means "Sorrowful Way."
3. When we pray the Stations of the Cross, we are granted graces and indulgences.
4. Jesus suffered through them because He loves us.

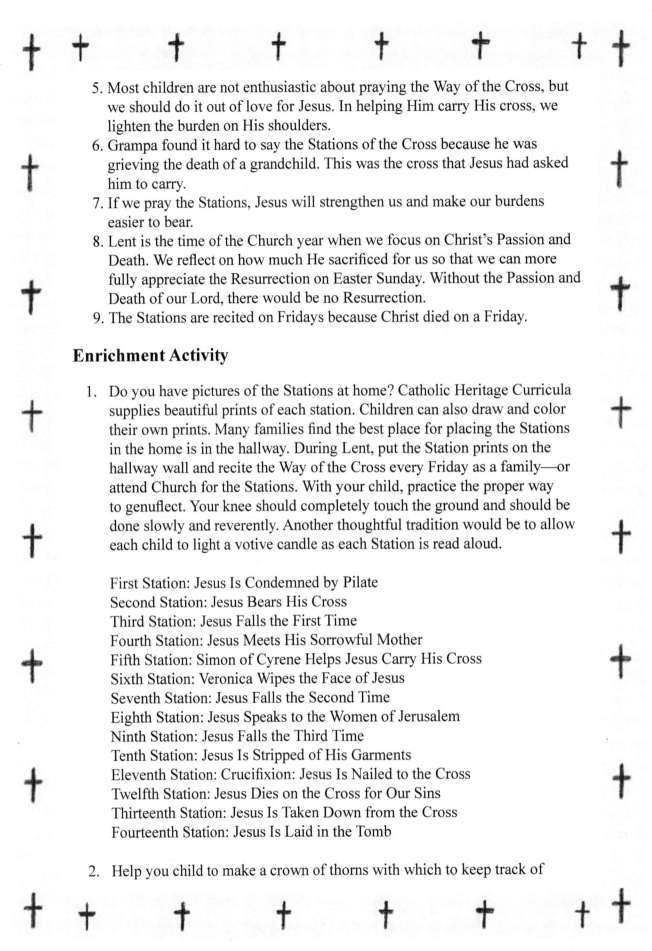

5. Most children are not enthusiastic about praying the Way of the Cross, but we should do it out of love for Jesus. In helping Him carry His cross, we lighten the burden on His shoulders.

6. Grampa found it hard to say the Stations of the Cross because he was grieving the death of a grandchild. This was the cross that Jesus had asked him to carry.

7. If we pray the Stations, Jesus will strengthen us and make our burdens easier to bear.

8. Lent is the time of the Church year when we focus on Christ's Passion and Death. We reflect on how much He sacrificed for us so that we can more fully appreciate the Resurrection on Easter Sunday. Without the Passion and Death of our Lord, there would be no Resurrection.

9. The Stations are recited on Fridays because Christ died on a Friday.

Enrichment Activity

1. Do you have pictures of the Stations at home? Catholic Heritage Curricula supplies beautiful prints of each station. Children can also draw and color their own prints. Many families find the best place for placing the Stations in the home is in the hallway. During Lent, put the Station prints on the hallway wall and recite the Way of the Cross every Friday as a family—or attend Church for the Stations. With your child, practice the proper way to genuflect. Your knee should completely touch the ground and should be done slowly and reverently. Another thoughtful tradition would be to allow each child to light a votive candle as each Station is read aloud.

   First Station: Jesus Is Condemned by Pilate
   Second Station: Jesus Bears His Cross
   Third Station: Jesus Falls the First Time
   Fourth Station: Jesus Meets His Sorrowful Mother
   Fifth Station: Simon of Cyrene Helps Jesus Carry His Cross
   Sixth Station: Veronica Wipes the Face of Jesus
   Seventh Station: Jesus Falls the Second Time
   Eighth Station: Jesus Speaks to the Women of Jerusalem
   Ninth Station: Jesus Falls the Third Time
   Tenth Station: Jesus Is Stripped of His Garments
   Eleventh Station: Crucifixion: Jesus Is Nailed to the Cross
   Twelfth Station: Jesus Dies on the Cross for Our Sins
   Thirteenth Station: Jesus Is Taken Down from the Cross
   Fourteenth Station: Jesus Is Laid in the Tomb

2. Help you child to make a crown of thorns with which to keep track of

Lenten sacrifices.

a. Using clay or Playdoh® roll out three long ropes. The longer the ropes the larger the crown is. Attach three ropes of clay together at the top and braid the ropes together. Connect the two ends into an enclosed circle. Place toothpicks in the crown and you have a crown of thorns.

b. The child removes a toothpick for each sacrifice or good deed he/she does during Lent.

c. On Easter morning hopefully all the toothpicks have been removed. The parent should place silk flowers in the holes left behind by the toothpicks.

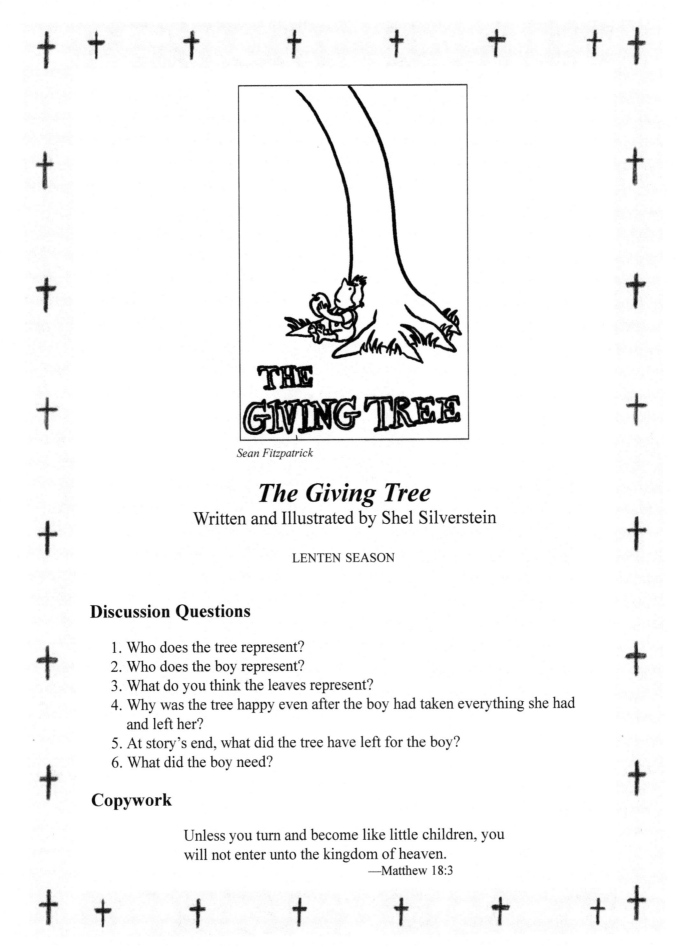

Sean Fitzpatrick

The Giving Tree
Written and Illustrated by Shel Silverstein

LENTEN SEASON

Discussion Questions

1. Who does the tree represent?
2. Who does the boy represent?
3. What do you think the leaves represent?
4. Why was the tree happy even after the boy had taken everything she had and left her?
5. At story's end, what did the tree have left for the boy?
6. What did the boy need?

Copywork

Unless you turn and become like little children, you
will not enter unto the kingdom of heaven.
—Matthew 18:3

Be still, and know that I am God.

—Psalm 46:10

Parent's Help Page
The Giving Tree

Observation

The tree gave the boy:
1. her apples for money;
2. branches for a house;
3. tree trunk for a boat.

Discussion Answers

1. The tree could represents God. He is strong and mighty. He gives to us what we need. He protects us and wants us to be happy.
2. The boy represents each of us. When we are young, we love and trust in God. As we grow up, sometimes we move away from God. But God is always waiting for us to come back to Him, desiring that we trust and love Him as we did when we were children.
3. The leaves on the tree could represent all the things that God gives us: food, water, shelter, family, and so on.
4. Even after the little boy had taken everything the tree had to offer, the tree was still happy because the little boy was happy.
5. At the end of the story, the tree had nothing left to give the boy except a "quiet place to sit and rest."
6. The boy needed to rest in God's peace. In the end, he realized how to "be still' and rest. God wants to give us many things. He wants to see us happy. He always wants us to approach Him as a little child would, full of love and trust. He wants us to "Be still, and know that [He is] God." He wants us to rest in His peace.

Enrichment Activity

Using green construction paper, cut many tree leaves. Then cut red apple shapes out of red construction paper. Each day, allow the child to write on a leaf or apple one thing that he is thankful to God for. Make a "giving tree" out of brown paper, and glue one leaf to the tree's branches each day until it is full.

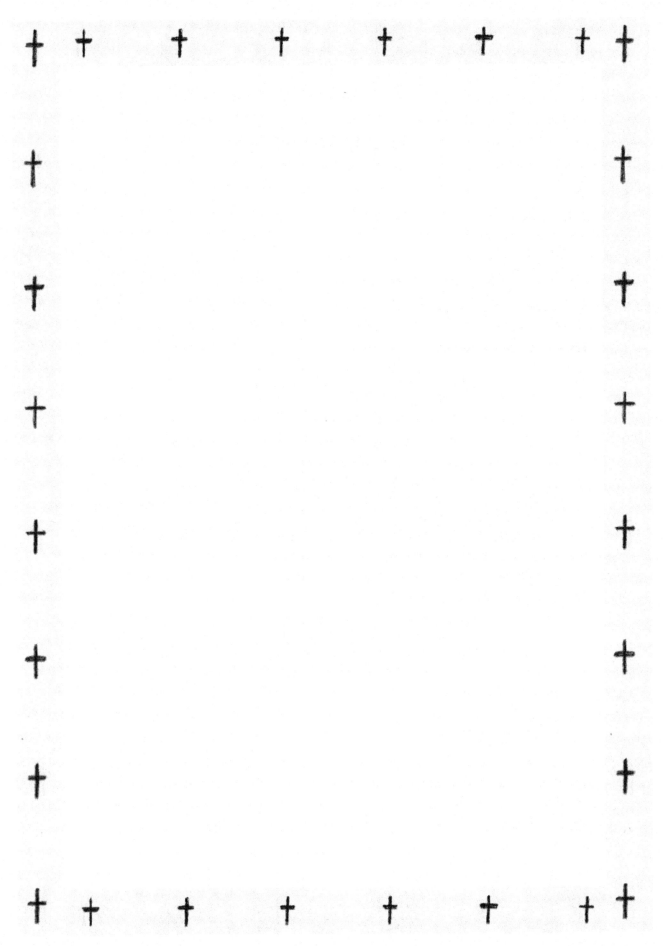

April

Sean Fitzpatrick

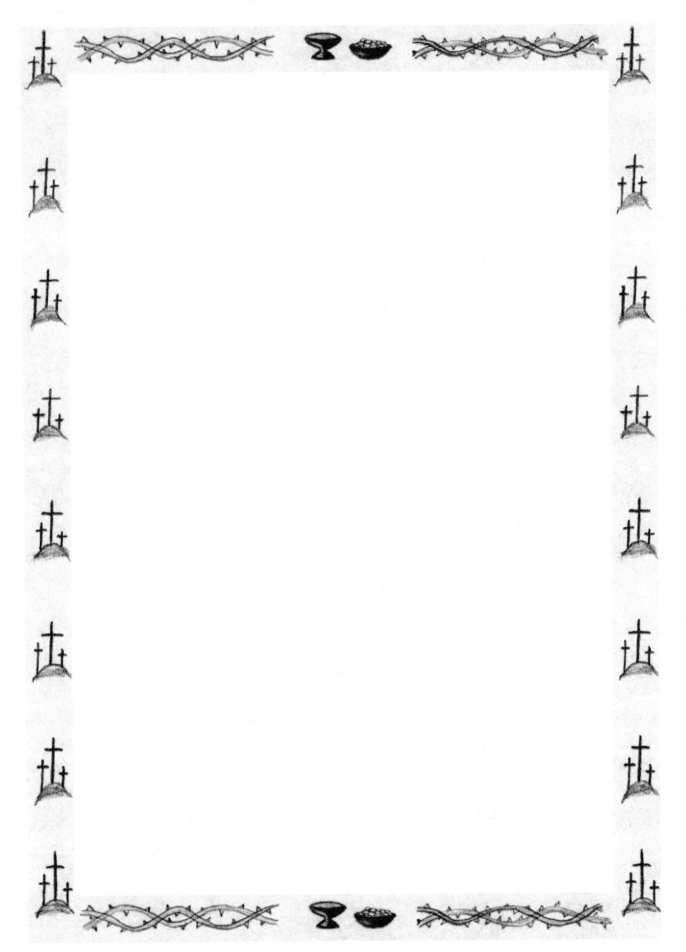

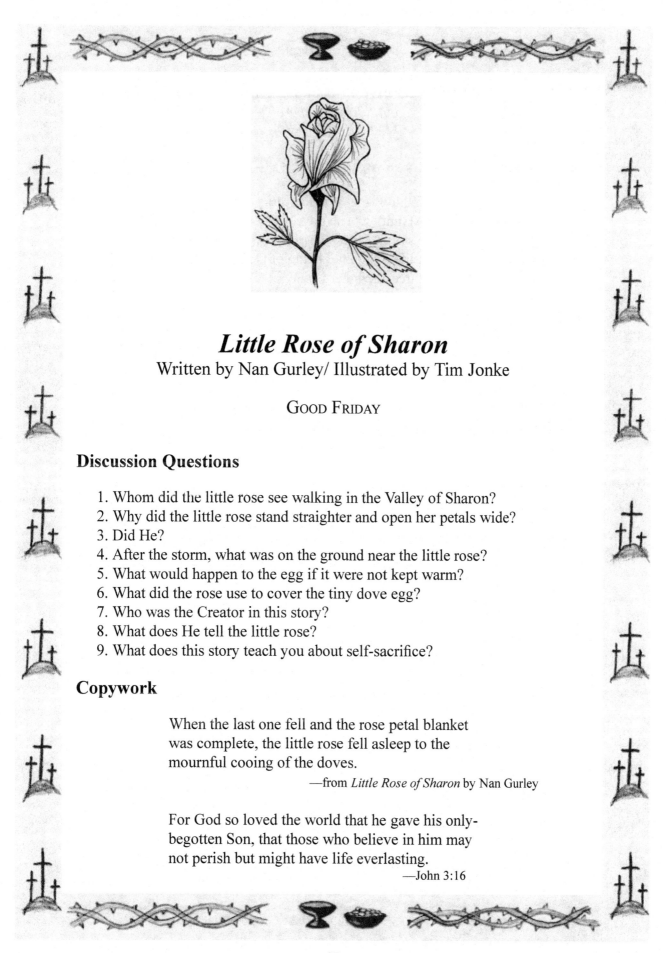

Little Rose of Sharon
Written by Nan Gurley/ Illustrated by Tim Jonke

GOOD FRIDAY

Discussion Questions

1. Whom did the little rose see walking in the Valley of Sharon?
2. Why did the little rose stand straighter and open her petals wide?
3. Did He?
4. After the storm, what was on the ground near the little rose?
5. What would happen to the egg if it were not kept warm?
6. What did the rose use to cover the tiny dove egg?
7. Who was the Creator in this story?
8. What does He tell the little rose?
9. What does this story teach you about self-sacrifice?

Copywork

> When the last one fell and the rose petal blanket
> was complete, the little rose fell asleep to the
> mournful cooing of the doves.
>
> —from *Little Rose of Sharon* by Nan Gurley

> For God so loved the world that he gave his only-
> begotten Son, that those who believe in him may
> not perish but might have life everlasting.
>
> —John 3:16

Parent's Help Page
Little Rose of Sharon

Observation

1. What other form of creation is used in this story to represent the Third Person of the Blessed Trinity? (The dove)
2. Notice that during the storm, the rose was not willing to sacrifice its beauty; but, for the safety and life of another being of God's creation, she willing sacrificed her greatest treasure—her beauty.

Discussion Answers

1. The little rose saw the Creator walking in the Valley of Sharon.
2. The little rose was hoping the Creator would notice her.
3. Yes.
4. The tiny dove's egg was on the ground near the rose.
5. If the egg was not kept warm, the baby dove would die.
6. The rose used her flower petals to cover the egg.
7. The Creator was God our Father.
8. He tells the little rose that one day His Son would give up everything He has as well and, because of the love the little rose showed the baby dove, His son would be called "My Son, the Rose of Sharon."
9. Let your child share his feelings about self-sacrifice. This is a chance for the parent to merely listen and let the child explore this valuable message of Christ and His love for each of us.

Enrichment Activities

1. Locate the Mediterranean Sea on a map or globe. Then label it on your map.
2. On separate index cards, list the flowers and trees found in the Valley of Sharon. Find a picture of these flowers and trees in magazines or on the Internet. Cut out the pictures and glue them onto the index cards.
   - rose
   - daffodil
   - almond tree
   - myrtle blossom
   - fig tree
   - olive tree
3. On a sheet of paper, glue a large picture of a red rose. Across the top, write the words Rose of Sharon and trace over the letters with a glue pen and then add glitter. Your copywork can also be included on this sheet.

Decorate your picture and add it to your Liturgical Year Notebook.

Easter is for Me!
Written by Dandi Daley Mackall/ Illustrated by Anton Petrov
Published by Concordia Publishing House, 2007.

Vocabulary

lame   Savior   eternal   mystery

Discussion Questions

1. What are the things you like best about Easter?
2. When was Jesus thinking of you?
3. When was Jesus speaking to you?
4. When was Jesus fishing for you?
5. Why did Jesus want to heal you?

6. Who did Jesus promise eternal life to?
7. When did Jesus pray for you?
8. When did Jesus suffer for you?
9. Why did Jesus do what He did?
10. What do we call Jesus' plan of dying for us and our salvation?
11. What day did Jesus rise again?

Copywork

Allow your child to select any rhyming verse from the book to copy in his best handwriting. Let him decorate his paper with Easter stickers.

Parent's Help Page
Easter is for Me!

Observation

Enjoy just looking at the pictures with your child. Allow him to notice things and ask questions. Which is his favorite picture? Which is his least favorite? Why? The pictures are beautiful and worth taking the time to meditate over and enjoy together.

Discussion Answers

1. Listen carefully to your child's answer and engage him in a conversation.
2. He was thinking of us when He was born and when he was playing.
3. He was speaking to us when He spoke God's word.
4. He was fishing for us when He fished with his friends.
5. He wanted to heal us because He loved and cared for everyone.
6 Jesus promised eternal life to ME!
7. He prayed for us when He prayed in the garden.
8. Jesus suffered for me when they beat Him and mocked Him and knocked Him down.
9. Jesus did what He did for love of me.
10. We call it a mystery.
11. Jesus rose again on Easter Sunday.

Enrichment Activity

Duplicate the cover of the book. Find a picture of your child and photographs of his cousins and friends. Paste the photos along the border of a nice, colored paper. At the top of the page, stencil in large letters "Easter is for Me!" In the center of the paper, paste a picture of the Resurrected Christ. Add pretty, colorful springtime and Easter stickers to the page for color and beauty.

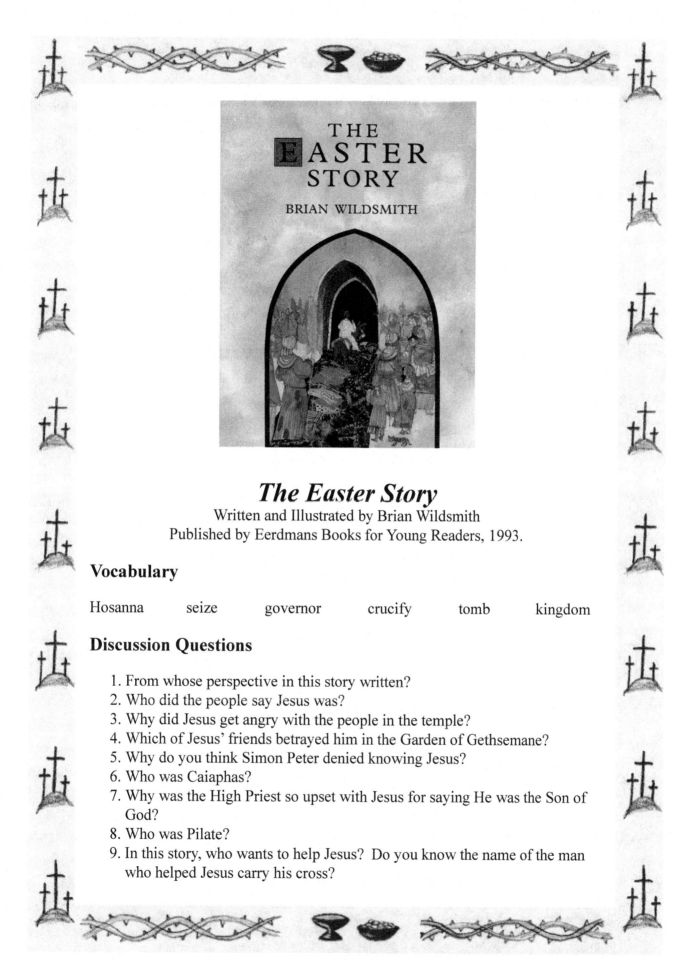

The Easter Story

Written and Illustrated by Brian Wildsmith
Published by Eerdmans Books for Young Readers, 1993.

Vocabulary

Hosanna   seize   governor   crucify   tomb   kingdom

Discussion Questions

1. From whose perspective in this story written?
2. Who did the people say Jesus was?
3. Why did Jesus get angry with the people in the temple?
4. Which of Jesus' friends betrayed him in the Garden of Gethsemane?
5. Why do you think Simon Peter denied knowing Jesus?
6. Who was Caiaphas?
7. Why was the High Priest so upset with Jesus for saying He was the Son of God?
8. Who was Pilate?
9. In this story, who wants to help Jesus? Do you know the name of the man who helped Jesus carry his cross?

10. What was the last thing the donkey did for Jesus?
11. Who did the women see when they went to the tomb on Easter morning?
12. Why do you think Jesus stayed on earth with His friends after rising from the dead?

Copywork

"Take and eat this," said Jesus, holding the bread.
"It is my body." Jesus lifted up a cup of wine.
"Take and drink this," Jesus said. "It is my blood."

—From the *The Easter Story*

Parent's Help Page
The Easter Story

Observation

1. There is an angel on every page of this book. Can you find each one? How does the artist Brian Wildsmith make his angels different from the ones usually seen in books? (Note all the colorful, versus the traditional white, robed figures.) Ask your child which angel—colorful or white—he prefers. Ask him to explain his choice.
2. Why do you think the author Brian Wildsmith told this story from a donkey's perspective? Discuss with your child how often a donkey is mentioned in Scripture. (Mary rides a donkey to Bethlehem before giving birth to Jesus. Jesus rides a donkey into Jerusalem on Palm Sunday. You might want to point out to your child that donkeys were a main source of transportation in Jesus' day.)

Discussion Answers

1. This book is written from the donkey's perspective.
2. The people said that Jesus was "the man who comes from God" and "the prophet Jesus from Nazareth in Galilee."
3. Jesus got angry because they were buying and selling things in God's house as though it were a market place.
4. Judas betrayed Jesus.
5. Answers will vary. Be sure that the child has time to explain his thoughts. You want to discuss the fear that Peter must have felt. Some children might feel upset with Peter for his denial.
6. Caiaphas was the High Priest of the Temple.

7. The High Priest considered it blasphemous language which is when someone says something very disrespectful about God or something sacred.
8. Pilate was the Roman governor.
9. The donkey wanted to help Jesus. Simon the Cyrene is the man who helped Jesus carry His cross.
9. The donkey carried Jesus' body to the tomb.
10. The women saw two angels at Jesus' tomb.
11. Answers will vary. Be sure the child has time to explain his answer. Probe for deeper answers as needed.

Enrichment Activities

1. Locate a map of Galilee. Locate Bethany. In the Gospel of John, it is reported that Jesus visited Lazarus (whom he had raised from death) before going on to Jerusalem where he was greeted with palms. Trace a path from Bethany to Jerusalem.
2. Donkeys in the life of Jesus: Create large timeline of the life of Jesus. (Use a lapbook or tape together several pieces of paper.) Cut pictures or draw scenes from the life of Jesus. Place them in order on the timeline or lapbook. Use the donkey pattern (below) and have the child move the donkey along the timeline, narrating the events from the life of Jesus as if the donkey is telling the story.
3. Create an Easter centerpiece. Materials needed: green Styrofoam ball; 2 popsicles/craft sticks painted brown; a 10×2 inch piece of purple fabric and a 10×2 inch piece of white fabric; Easter stickers or flower stickers or small plastic flowers.

Cut the Styrofoam in half. Place it on the table with the cut side down making a green mound. Glue the popsicles sticks into the shape of the cross. Place the cross in the mound making it stand securely in place. Drape the purple and white cloths from one side of the cross to the other. Decorate the mound with stickers or flowers. To make this centerpiece remind the child of the story Wildsmith created, use the donkey pattern as a template and glue or attach it to the mound at the foot of the cross.

You might want to follow up this story with the book by Marisa Mignolli *Hosanna to You, Jesus!* It also features a donkey in the story.

St. George and the Dragon

Retold by Margaret Hodges/ Illustrated by Trina Schart Hyman
Published by Brown Little Publishers, 1984.

Cover reprinted by permission of the publisher.

FEAST DAY: ST. GEORGE APRIL 23

Vocabulary

champion	hermit	bade	anvil	brimstone
perils	victorious	furnace	monstrous	wrathful
vast	bellow	devour	scorch	prey
brandish	sever	barb	lark	tambourine

Discussion Questions

1. What was the princess's sorrow?
2. What does the name "George" mean?
3. Who is the Red Cross Knight known as today?
4. What do you think of the author's description of the dragon? Listen to it again and think about it.
5. In fairy tales, what do you think dragons represent?
6. What does the knight lie in/under each night that gives him rest and recovery?
7. Why didn't the Red Cross Knight accept the king's offer to "stay here and live happily ever after"?
8. What did the Red Cross Knight accept as his reward instead?

Copywork

Allow your child to select his/her own copywork selection. Perhaps boys would like to copy part of the description of the dragon. If they cannot find a suitable selection, King Edward's motto is a good option: "*Honi Soit Qui Mal y Pense,*" or "Shamed be the person who thinks evil of it"

Parent's Help Page
St. George and the Dragon

Observation

Go through the book with your child and observe the illustrations. Trina Schart Hyman's magnificent art work is a study in art appreciation.

In England's history, St. George represented the ideal knight. He was courageous, honest, gallant, and honorable. Notice St. George's shield in Hyman's artwork. It has a large red cross upon it. This was a symbol of the Crusades, the battles the Christians fought to take back the holy land (Jerusalem) from the Muslims. The Crusades lasted for over 200 years and there are many stories, folklores, and songs about the famous Crusades.

Reread the page where the Red Cross Knight is on the hilltop with the hermit. Pay special attention to the description of the "mountaintop that touched the highest heavens" and the palace atop it. What are the angels doing? Point out the angels as you read this to your child. Where does the Red Cross Knight tell the hermit he would rather go? And what does the hermit tell him? Reread the hermit's words to the Red Cross Knight while explaining to your child that though we would prefer to go into the beautiful palace atop the mountain, we, as Christians, have been called to "go down into the valley and fight the dragon that [we] were sent to fight." Boys and men are soldiers for Christ, just like the Red Cross Knight.

Now have your child notice what Una does as she watches the Red Cross Knight get wounded as he valiantly fights the dragon. As he falls down, she falls to her knees in prayer. Girls and women are prayer warriors for Christ, just like Una. Our prayers and vigilant watch strengthen the soldiers of Christ to "fight the good fight" so that we can all "hang our shield" on the palace wall where the heavenly angels fly.

At the end of the story, the illustrator Trina Schart Hyman has included shields at the four corners of the page. Notice the red cross on the shields. Each shield has something written inside of it:

> Bottom left: 1984 is the copyright date
> Bottom right: Engraving of the illustrator's name
> The two top shields bear a French motto: *"Honi Soit Qui Mal y Pense"* which, translated into English, reads: "Shamed be the person who thinks evil of it." This was the motto of King Edward III, a very popular king of medieval England.

Discussion Answers

1. The dragon was the princess's sorrow.
2. The name George means "plow the earth" and "fight the good fight."
3. Today the Red Cross Knight is known as St. George.
4. Reread the description of the dragon back to the child and get his opinion. Do not give your opinion—merely listen to your child's answer and see the dragon through his eyes.
5. The knight lay under "an ancient spring of silvery water" and "a fair apple tree" that "dropped a healing dew."
6. In fairy tales, the dragon represents some sort of evil.
7. The Red Cross Knight did not accept the king's offer because he said he still owed the Fairy Queen his knight's service.
8. Instead, the Red Cross Knight accepted Una's hand in marriage.

The Little Caterpillar That Finds Jesus
~ A Parable of the Eucharist ~
Written and Illustrated by Susan Andrew Brindle/Miriam Andrews
Lademan/ Joan Andrews Bell
Published by Precious Life Books, Inc, 2004.
Cover reprinted by permission of the publisher.

ADORATION

Vocabulary

original	adoration	consume	penetrate
pang	redemptive	monstrance	procession
transform	multitude	gratitude	chalice
consecration	indifference	console	

Discussion Answers

1. Did Gloriana think about Jesus very much when she lived in the garden? Why not?
2. Why did Gloriana finally call out to Jesus?
3. Where did the children bring the vase of flowers?
4. While in the chapel, what did Gloriana realize?
5. What were the little boy and girl instructed to do when they adore Christ?
6. Where did Gloriana find Jesus?
7. Did Jesus' friends understand what He meant about giving them His flesh and blood?
8. On the page where Jesus is talking to the crowd, why did He not call them back and explain that He had mistakenly told them it was His body and blood?
9. What transformed Gloriana and how was she physically transformed?
10. Why is Jesus lonely?

Copywork

Jesus, I love You and I adore You!
—prayer in *The Little Caterpillar That Finds Jesus*

He who eats My flesh and drinks My blood, abides
in Me and I in him.
—John 6:55

Parent's Help Page
The Little Caterpillar That Finds Jesus

Observation

1. Observe the page that depicts all the children entering the church. What is taking place? (First Communion)
2. Go through the book and look at the pictures of the Consecrated Host. Who (Jesus) or what (cross) is drawn inside the host? Why do you think the illustrator has done that?

Discussion Answers

1. No, Gloriana didn't think much about Jesus. She knew of Him but she was comfortable and content in her little garden. Besides, Jesus seemed far away.

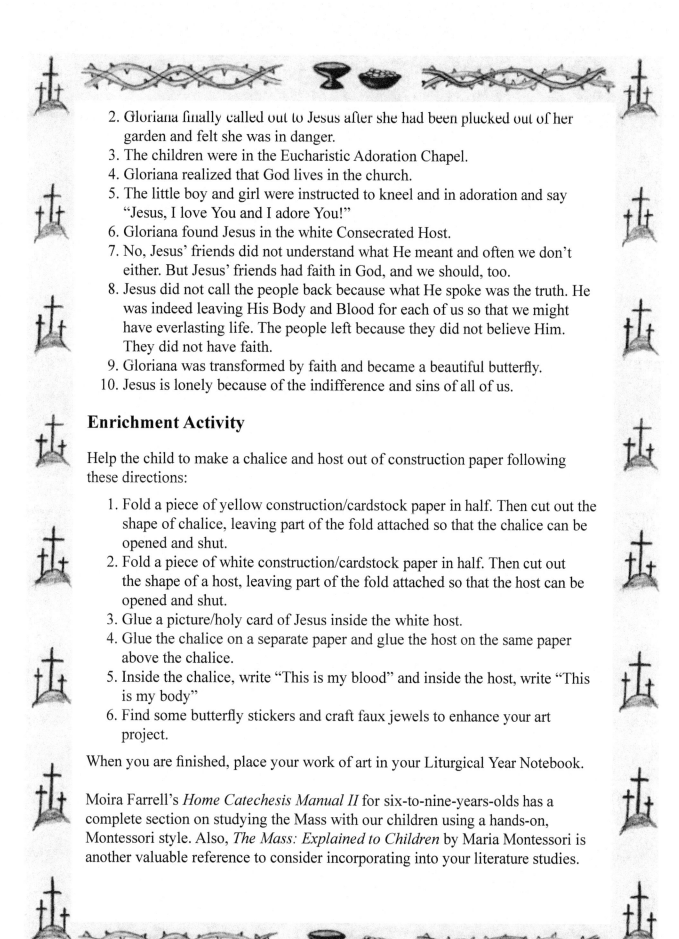

2. Gloriana finally called out to Jesus after she had been plucked out of her garden and felt she was in danger.
3. The children were in the Eucharistic Adoration Chapel.
4. Gloriana realized that God lives in the church.
5. The little boy and girl were instructed to kneel and in adoration and say "Jesus, I love You and I adore You!"
6. Gloriana found Jesus in the white Consecrated Host.
7. No, Jesus' friends did not understand what He meant and often we don't either. But Jesus' friends had faith in God, and we should, too.
8. Jesus did not call the people back because what He spoke was the truth. He was indeed leaving His Body and Blood for each of us so that we might have everlasting life. The people left because they did not believe Him. They did not have faith.
9. Gloriana was transformed by faith and became a beautiful butterfly.
10. Jesus is lonely because of the indifference and sins of all of us.

Enrichment Activity

Help the child to make a chalice and host out of construction paper following these directions:

1. Fold a piece of yellow construction/cardstock paper in half. Then cut out the shape of chalice, leaving part of the fold attached so that the chalice can be opened and shut.
2. Fold a piece of white construction/cardstock paper in half. Then cut out the shape of a host, leaving part of the fold attached so that the host can be opened and shut.
3. Glue a picture/holy card of Jesus inside the white host.
4. Glue the chalice on a separate paper and glue the host on the same paper above the chalice.
5. Inside the chalice, write "This is my blood" and inside the host, write "This is my body"
6. Find some butterfly stickers and craft faux jewels to enhance your art project.

When you are finished, place your work of art in your Liturgical Year Notebook.

Moira Farrell's *Home Catechesis Manual II* for six-to-nine-years-olds has a complete section on studying the Mass with our children using a hands-on, Montessori style. Also, *The Mass: Explained to Children* by Maria Montessori is another valuable reference to consider incorporating into your literature studies.

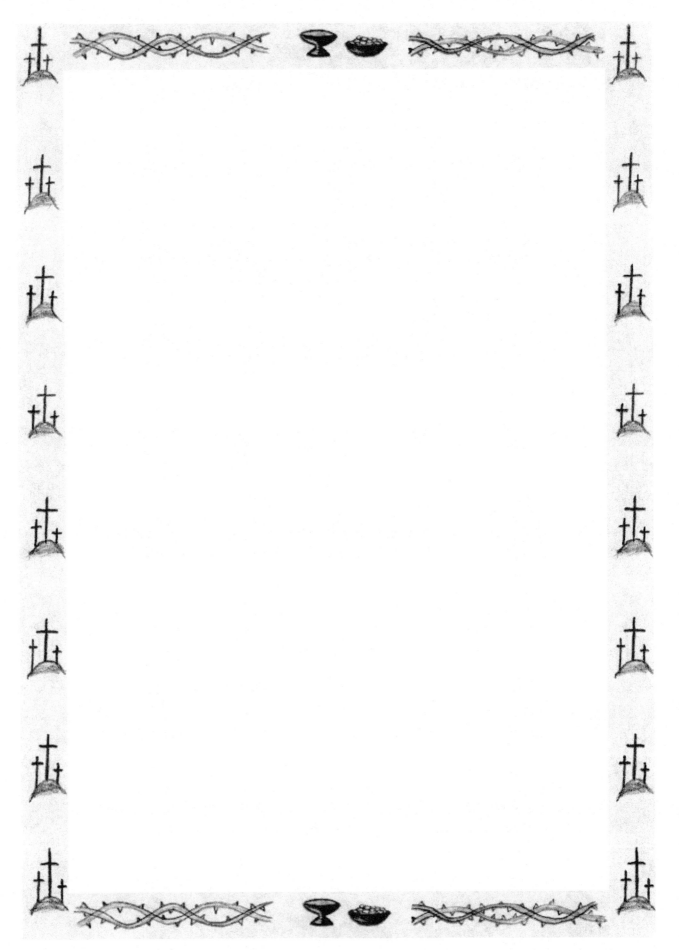

May

Sean Fitzpatrick

Lovely Lady Dressed in Blue
~ and the Knights of Our Lady ~

Written and Illustrated by Joan Andrews Bell/ Susan Andrews Brindle/
Miriam Andrews Lademan
Published by Precious Life Books, Inc, 2004.
Cover reprinted by permission of the publisher.

MONTH OF MAY: MARIAN DEVOTION

Vocabulary

nicker	champion	cohort	persecuted	condemn
crevice	villainous	downtrodden	chivalry	chivalrous
wistful	allegiance	consecrate	dedicate	lull
homage	heretic	austerity	defy	infinite
pensive	persist	secure	sanctuary	eternity

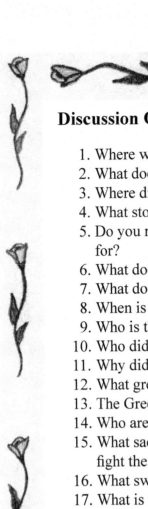

Discussion Questions

1. Where were the children and Aunt Miriam going?
2. What does the horse's name, Ruah, mean?
3. Where did Aunt Miriam take the children?
4. What storybook did the children pretend to be in the woods?
5. Do you remember what Robin Hood and his merry men were best known for?
6. What does the word "Friar" mean?
7. What does the word "Catholic" mean?
8. When is chivalry still found today?
9. Who is the "King of Kings" and the "fairest Queen of all"?
10. Who did the children vow their allegiance to?
11. Why did the knightly children stop at the church on their way home?
12. What great saint defended the Faith as a Knight for God?
13. The Greek word 'heresy' means what?
14. Who are the two victims of abortion?
15. What sacrament gives us the strength, purity, and consoling that we need to fight the good fight?
16. What sword did St. Dominic use to fight for Christ against the Albigenses?
17. What is the miracle of the Incarnation?
18. What do you think will bring a change in people's hearts and end abortion?

Copywork

Thank you, Dear Jesus, for home and family.
—words of Aunt Miriam in *Lovely Lady Dressed in Blue*

Parent's Help Page
Lovely Lady Dressed in Blue

Observation

1. Observe the picture of Aunt Miriam making peanut butter and jelly sandwiches for the children at the kitchen table. What do you think the words *Laudetur Jesus Christus* over the fireplace mantle mean? (These words stand for Praised be Jesus Christ!)
2. The Albigenses were heretics in Southern France. Locate Southern France on a map or globe.

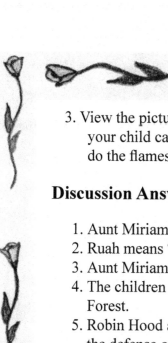

3. View the picture of Mary and the twelve Apostles in the upper room. See if your child can explain how they felt after you read page 41 to them. What do the flames of fire over their head represent?

Discussion Answers

1. Aunt Miriam and the children were going on a long journey.
2. Ruah means "breath of wind."
3. Aunt Miriam took the children to a secret hideout in the woods.
4. The children pretended to be Robin Hood and his merry men in Sherwood Forest.
5. Robin Hood and his merry men were best known for "virtues of loyalty, and the defense of the downtrodden."
6. 'Friar' means 'Brother'.
7. 'Catholic' means 'Universal'.
8. Chivalry is still found today when we "treat others with respect, kindness, and love."
9. Christ is the one true King and Mary is the fairest Queen of all.
10. The children vowed their allegiance to Jesus Christ and the Blessed Mother.
11. They stopped at the church to pay homage to their King.
12. St. Dominic became a Knight for God.
13. The Greek word 'heresy' means 'choice'.
14. The two victims of abortion are the baby and the mother.
15. The Sacrament of Confirmation gives us the graces we need to fight the good fight.
16. St. Dominic used the Holy Rosary as his weapon to crusade for Christ.
17. The miracle of the Incarnation was God coming to earth as a newborn baby.
18. The Rosary will bring about a change in people's hearts and end abortion.

Enrichment Activities

1. Pro-life areas to address with your children, *depending upon age-level*:
   - Abortion
   - Euthanasia
   - Care of Elderly
   - Care of Handicapped Children
   - Chastity
   - Natural Family Planning
2. Discuss with your child some ways to help those in crisis pregnancies and to encourage the sanctity of life:
   - Give informative talks or ask a pro-life speaker to speak at your church (get approval from your pastor first)

- work to change unjust and evil laws
- teach about the beauty of life
- open homes to women who are pregnant
- hand out literature
- peacefully and prayerfully seek to influence women away from abortion mills
- host a pro-life baby shower and give donations to your local pregnancy center
- host a Giving Tree at Christmas time at your church for baby donations
- host a pro-life march or attend a candlelight vigil on the anniversary of Roe vs. Wade January 22

Some ways that even very young children can help save babies:

- pray
- offer small sacrifices

Madonna of the Carnation by Luini Bernardino

The Weight of a Mass

Written by Josephine Nobisso/ Illustrated by Katalin Szegedi
Published by Gingerbread House, 2002.
Cover reprinted by permission of the publisher.

FIRST HOLY COMMUNION

Vocabulary

betroth	subjects	prosperous	taunt	marzipan
jaunty	confection	erect	miniscule	compel
probe	consent	propose	ceremonious	poach
union	shuffle	schilling	flair	snippet
bewilderment	teetered	diverse	stun	procession

Discussion Questions

1. How can we tell that the king was a good and holy man?
2. Why were the king's subjects not attending Mass regularly?
3. What did the widow ask for in the bakery? What was she able to pay?
4. What does the baker mean when he says that the young boy shares the same disease as the widow and his mother?
5. Describe how the baker tested the Mass intention.
6. What happened when the baker's son lifted the tiny slip of tissue paper?
7. What did the baker mean when he said he thought his son might exchange his apron for a white collar? Why do you think he thought that? Do you think he will be more willing to see his son a priest at the end of the story?
8. Why did everyone leave the bakery and go to the Cathedral?
9. Why did the old widow only take one slice of bread in exchange for a Mass intention?

Copywork

One Mass—I, too, do not know the weight of a Mass.

—the Widow in *Weight of a Mass*

Parent's Help Page
The Weight of a Mass

Observation

Parent and child should take time to just enjoy the beautiful art work by Katalin Szegedi. It's a joy to simply look through this book and delight in the rich treats and treasures found within its pages.

Discussion Answers

1. We know this because he agreed to be married in the cathedral even though he knew only a few old women would be in attendance.
2. The king's subjects were not attending Mass regularly because they had "grown cold and careless in the practice of their faith."
3. The widow asked for a crust of stale bread in exchange for one Mass said for the baker.

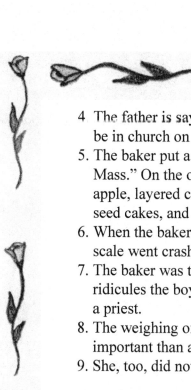

4. The father is saying that unless he is kept busy at the bakery, the boy would be in church on his knees.
5. The baker put a tiny slip of tissue paper on the scale with the words "One Mass." On the other side of the scale, he piled on old bread, a marzipan apple, layered cake, cherry-topped cupcakes, chocolates, a dozen poppy seed cakes, and two-dozen rolls.
6. When the baker's son lifted the tiny slip of tissue paper, the other side of the scale went crashing down.
7. The baker was thinking that maybe his son would become a priest. He ridicules the boy for this piety. Perhaps at the end he will let his son become a priest.
8. The weighing of the Mass showed all the people that the Mass was more important than anything else. They all went to the cathedral to go to Mass.
9. She, too, did not know the weight of a Mass.

Enrichment Activities

1. Visit the website of the lady who wrote *The Weight of a Mass*: http://www.gingerbreadbooks.com/
2. Study the cathedral in the picture. Find a picture of Notre Dame Cathedral and compare it to this author's illustration.
3. Bake a loaf of bread and then a rich cake with confection sugar. Compare the two by making a compare/contrast sheet. Include comparisons on sight, smell, and taste.
4. Compare/Contrast the *front* inside page of the book with the *back* inside page of the book. Notice all the differences in the two pictures. (Daylight streaming into the cathedral vs. moon, stars, and candles of night; the emptiness and solitude of the cathedral vs. the crowd and enthusiasm in the cathedral.)
5. Can you find a scale like the one in the book? If you can, practice weighing various objects on it.
6. For extra study ideas, go to: http://www.chcweb.com/catalog/files/womstudyguide.pdf

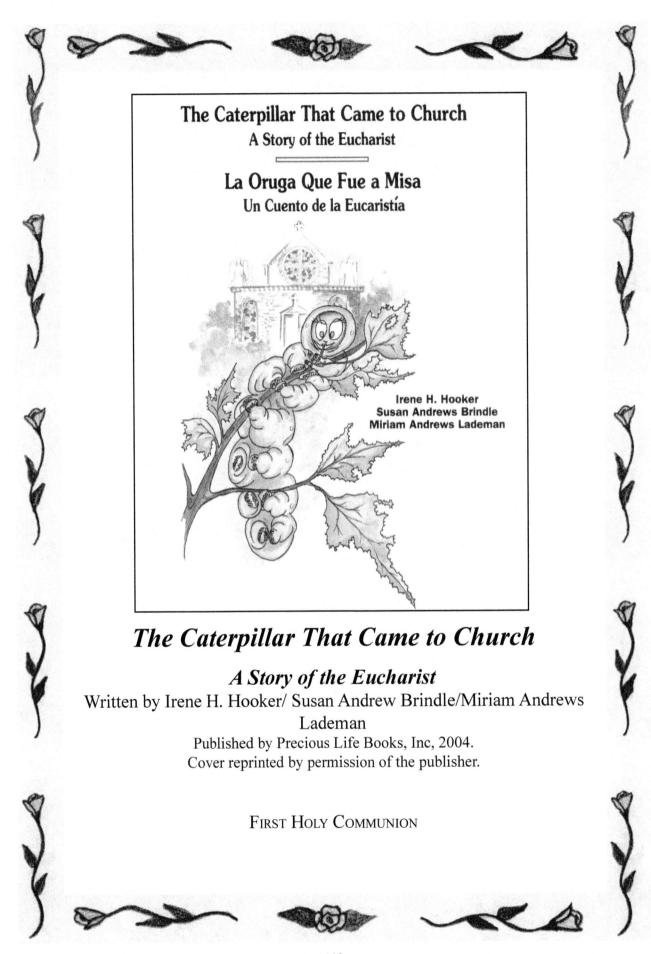

The Caterpillar That Came to Church
A Story of the Eucharist

La Oruga Que Fue a Misa
Un Cuento de la Eucaristía

Irene H. Hooker
Susan Andrews Brindle
Miriam Andrews Lademan

The Caterpillar That Came to Church

A Story of the Eucharist

Written by Irene H. Hooker/ Susan Andrew Brindle/Miriam Andrews
Lademan
Published by Precious Life Books, Inc, 2004.
Cover reprinted by permission of the publisher.

FIRST HOLY COMMUNION

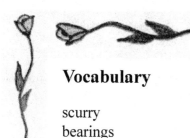
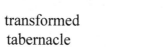

Vocabulary

scurry   transformed   consecration
bearings   tabernacle   supreme
sacrifice

Discussion Questions

1. Can you tell that the woman is Catholic just by looking at the content's of the woman's handbag? What are the clues?
2. Why was Mariana scared and lonely?
3. What did Mariana notice at the altar?
4 Why did Mariana cry?
5. Who else was around the altar, praising, praying, and singing to God?
6. What is the most profound moment of the Mass?
7. What is it called?
8. Who is really and truly present on the altar?
9. What made Mariana change into a beautiful butterfly?

Copywork

Always come to Me in love, so I can live in you.
Everything is possible through love.
—words of Jesus in *The Caterpillar That Came to Church*

Parent's Help Page

The Caterpillar That Came to Church

Observation

1. Compare the crucifix picture on page 32 with the picture on page 34.
2. Compare the Host in the picture on page 40 with the picture on page 42.

Discussion Answers

1. Allow your child to point out the objects. Make special mention of the prayer book and the rosary.
2. Mariana was scared because she felt alone and wanted to be free to go home.
3. Mariana noticed the priest, the crucifix, and the gold box.

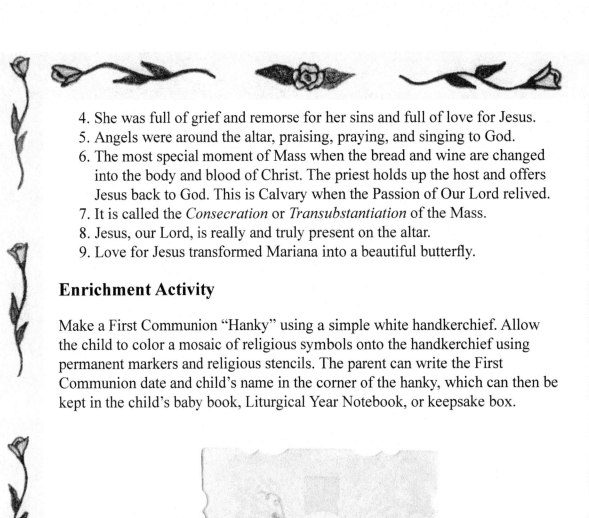

4. She was full of grief and remorse for her sins and full of love for Jesus.
5. Angels were around the altar, praising, praying, and singing to God.
6. The most special moment of Mass when the bread and wine are changed into the body and blood of Christ. The priest holds up the host and offers Jesus back to God. This is Calvary when the Passion of Our Lord relived.
7. It is called the *Consecration* or *Transubstantiation* of the Mass.
8. Jesus, our Lord, is really and truly present on the altar.
9. Love for Jesus transformed Mariana into a beautiful butterfly.

Enrichment Activity

Make a First Communion "Hanky" using a simple white handkerchief. Allow the child to color a mosaic of religious symbols onto the handkerchief using permanent markers and religious stencils. The parent can write the First Communion date and child's name in the corner of the hanky, which can then be kept in the child's baby book, Liturgical Year Notebook, or keepsake box.

Pascual and the Kitchen Angels
Written and Illustrated by Tomie dePaola

FEAST DAY: ST. PASCHAL BAYLON MAY 17

Vocabulary

garland   monastery   friars   habit

Discussion Questions

1. What did Pascual's parents think he was going to do with his life?
2. What monastery did Pascual's parents tell him to go to?
3. What did Pascual bring in his basket to the monastery?
4. What did Pascual do instead of cooking?
5. Why was he able to do that?
6. What did Pascual want to do? Did he get his wish?
7. What you do you think about angels? How do they help *you*?

Copywork

For to his angels he has given command about you,
that they guard you in all your ways.

—Psalms 90:11

Parent's Help Page
Pascual and the Kitchen Angels

Discussion Answers

1. Pascual's parents thought he would become a shepherd.
2. His parents told him to go to the Monastery of Saint Francis.
3. Pascual brought a basket of cheeses, eggs, flour, dried beans, vegetables, and fruit.
4. Instead of cooking, Pascual knelt down to pray.
5. The kitchen angels did the cooking.
6. Pascual wanted to feed hungry people. Yes, he got his wish.
7. Talk to your child about angels.

Enrichment Activities

1. See if you can draw a kitchen angel that looks like one of Tomie dePaola's.
2. See if your library has Tomie dePaola's new angel book: *Angels, Angels Everywhere* (Published by Penguin Young Reader's Group, 2005.)
3. Write or dictate your own story about an angel helping in your house.

Sean Fitzpatrick

Karol from Poland

Written by M. Leonora Wilson/ Illustrated by Carla Koch

POPE JOHN PAUL II: BIRTHDAY MAY 18TH

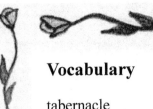

Vocabulary

tabernacle   university   sacred
cardinal   signal   missionary

Discussion Questions

1. When and where was Karol Wojtyla born?
2. What does the name "Karol" mean?
3. What are some things Karol enjoyed doing?
4. During what war did Karol live?
5. How long was John Paul I our pope?
6. When did John Paul II become Pope?
7. What does the word "Pope" mean?
8. Describe the "Popemobile."
9. Describe what happened to the Pope on May 13, 1981?
10. How did Pope John Paul II treat the man who shot him?
11. What is a missionary?
12. Who is our new pope?

Copywork

Be not afraid.
— Pope John Paul II's first words as Pope

Parent's Help Page
Karol from Poland

Observation

As you look through this book and observe the pictures, notice things about Pope John Paul II's life that is similar to your own life. (For example, shopping with his mother, going to church, playing soccer, skiing with friends, reading, etc.)

How was his life different from yours?

Discussion Answers

1. Karol Wojtyla was born in Poland on May 18, 1920.
2. The name "Karol" means "Charles."
3. Karol enjoyed sports, especially soccer, putting on plays, hiking, fishing,

swimming, and skiing.

4. Karol lived through World War II.
5. Pope John Paul I was pope for only 33 days.
6. John Paul II became pope on October 16, 1978.
7. The word "Pope" means "Father."
8. The Popemobile was a white car with a glass encasement over the top.
9. On May 13, 1981, someone shot the pope.
10. A missionary is a "person who teaches other people about God."
11. Pope John Paul II forgave the man who shot him and even visited him in prison.
12. Pope Benedict XVI became the new pope.

Enrichment Activities

1. Locate Poland on a map of Europe. Label it on your world or Europe map.
2. *John Paul the Great Unit Study* by Nancy Brown, Maureen Wittmann, and Cay Gibson is available online at
   http://www.heart-and-mind.com/htdocs/archives/jpii_web_small.pdf or by request from *Heart and Mind Magazine* at PO Box 420881, San Diego, CA 92142

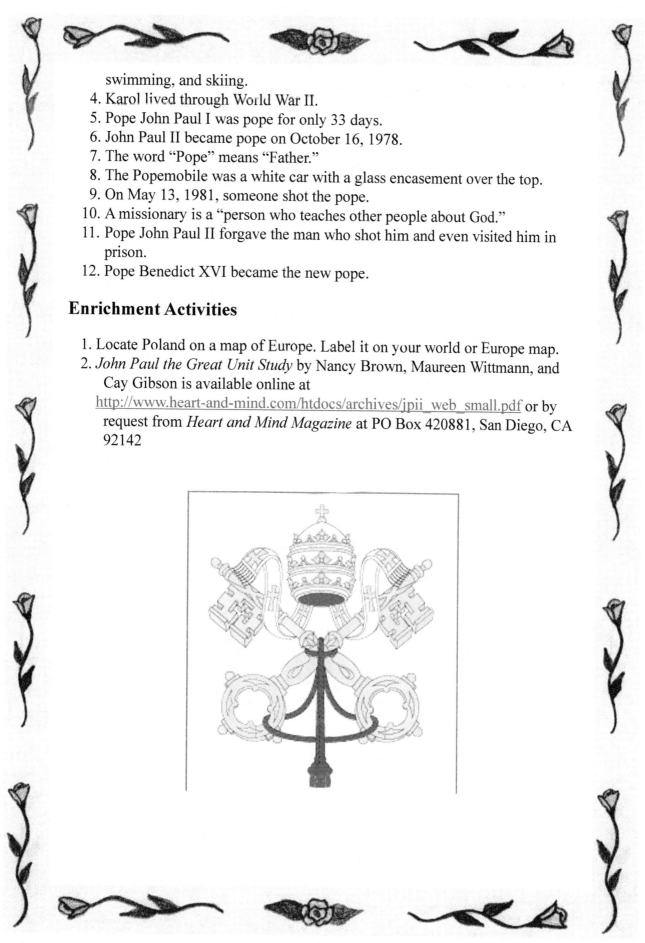

June

Sean Fitzpatrick

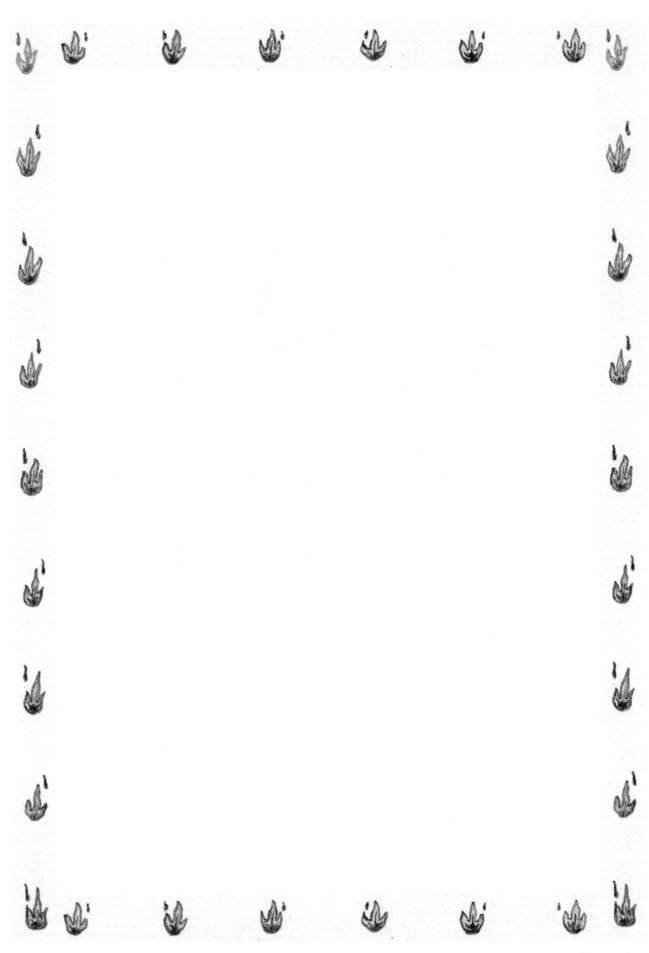

The Twelve Apostles
Written and Illustrated by Marianna Mayer

PENTECOST

Vocabulary

impulsive	prediction	descend	basilica	excavator
prophet	avenge	zeal	sect	zealot

Discussion Questions

1. What was the one important task Jesus entrusted to His apostles?
2. What does the word "apostle" mean?
3. Who was the first apostle mentioned in Scripture and what does his name mean?
4. What did the apostle Andrew do for a living?
5. Name three passages in Scripture where James the Elder is mention.
6. From the cross, what favor did Jesus ask of John?
7. What famous book of the Bible did St. John write?
8. Why is St. Matthew often depicted with a bag of coins or a moneybox?
9. What does the name "Philip" mean?
10. Why is St. Bartholomew often pictured together with a chained demon?
11. What is Jude Thaddeus the patron saint of?
12. It is believed that Simon was a member of what movement?
13. James the Younger is believed to have been the brother of which apostle?

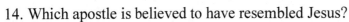

14. Which apostle is believed to have resembled Jesus?
15. How is St. Thomas best remembered and why?
16. Which apostle betrayed Jesus?
17. Who took the place of Judas?
18. Which apostles interested you the most?

Copywork

Come, follow me, and I will make you fishers of men.
—Matthew 4:19

My Lord and My God!
—traditional Eucharistic exclamation, attributed to St. Thomas
when he sees Christ after the Resurrection

Parent's Help Page
The Twelve Apostles

Observation

Observe the pictures of Jesus' friends and watch for pictures of them in other art
holding their designated symbols

St. Peter—keys, cockerel
St. Andrew—cross in the shape of an X and sometimes a fish
St. James the Elder—sword, bishop's hat
St. John—eagle, book
St. Matthew—bag of coins, desk with an angel, pen, inkwell, moneybox
St. Philip—loaves of bread or tall cross
St. Bartholomew—a knife blade
St. Jude Thaddeus—a gold sailing ship
St. Simon—book
St. James the Younger—a club or book
St. Thomas—T-square
St. Matthias—the ax

Discussion Answers

1. The task Jesus entrusted to His apostles was "to announce the Good News."
2. The word "apostle" is derived from a Greek word meaning "one who is sent out."
3. Peter was the first apostle mentioned in Scripture. His name means "rock."
4. The apostle Andrew was a fisherman.
5. James the Elder is mentioned 1) when Jesus raised Jairus' daughter, 2) as being on the Mount of Transfiguration, and 3) as being in the Garden of Gethsemane.

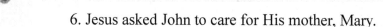

6. Jesus asked John to care for His mother, Mary.

7. It is believed that St. John wrote the Book of Revelations.

8. St. Matthew was a tax collector before he became a follower of Jesus.

9. The name Philip is a Greek word meaning "he who loves horses."

10. St. Bartholomew is pictured with a chained demon because he is known for healing the sick and for having banished a demon from an idol.

11. Jude Thaddeus is the patron saint of Lost Causes.

12. It is believed that Simon was a member of the Zealot movement (a religious sect of "freedom fighters").

13. James the Younger is believed to have been the brother of Matthew.

14. James the Younger is believed to have resembled Jesus.

15. St. Thomas is best remembered as "Doubting Thomas" because he would not believe in the risen Christ until "I see the holes the nails made in his hands, put my finger on the nailmarks and my hand into his side."

16. Judas betrayed Jesus.

17. Matthias took Judas' place among the fellowship of the Twelve Apostles.

Enrichment Activities

1. Name the twelve Apostles. Then, on a calendar, write each apostle's name on his feast day:
   - St. Peter—June 29
   - St. Andrew—November 30
   - St. James the Elder—July 25
   - St. John—December 27
   - St. Matthew—September 21
   - St. Philip—May 1
   - St. Bartholomew—August 24
   - St. Jude Thaddeus—October 28
   - St. Simon—October 28
   - St. James the Younger—May 3
   - St. Thomas—July 3
   - St. Matthias—May 14

2. Find a copy of Leonardo Da Vinci's famous painting *The Last Supper* and try to discern which apostle is which. Remember, St. Matthias is not in this painting as he replaced Judas.

   Find the figure holding the bag of coins. Do you think this might be Judas, the traitor who sold Christ to the soldiers for 30 pieces of silver, or St. Matthew, the former tax collector? Explain your answer.

3. Choose one apostle who interests the you the most. Research his life and write or dictate a paragraph about him.

Maureen Van Nostrand

The Princess and the Kiss
Written by Jennie Bishop/ Illustrated by Preston McDaniels

JUNE: COURTSHIP AND WEDDINGS

Vocabulary

splendor   elegant   amazement
cherish   magnificent   suitor

Discussion Questions

1. What gift did the king and queen give their daughter when she was born?
2. Who was the kiss from?
3. Describe each suitor and explain why the princess sent each one away.
4. Why was the common boy from the fields finally the right match for the princess?
5. How had the prince and princess wisely protected the gift entrusted to them by God?

Copywork

Love comes from a pure heart and a good
conscience and a sincere faith.

—adapted from 1 Timothy 1:5, printed
in the book *The Princess and the Kiss*

Parent's Help Page
The Princess and the Kiss

Discussion Answers

1. The king and queen gave their daughter a kiss.
2. The kiss was from God.
3. The first suitor was Prince Peacock. He was too full of himself.
   The second suitor was Prince Romance. The princess felt he would lose
   interest in her kiss.
   The third suitor was Prince Treasurechest. He had so much; the princess felt
   her kiss would not be special to him.
4. He had saved his kiss for the princess, just as she had saved hers.
5. Allow the child to give his/her reason why.

Observation

The pictures in this book are a treasure. Take time to explore the pages and talk
about the drawings with your child.

Enrichment Activity

God has given you a very special gift. Your parents have kept it safe in their care
all these years. What is it? What will you do with it? Write your own story about
this gift, or tell it to your mom or dad so they can write it for you. Put your story
in your Liturgical Year Notebook.

Sean Fitzpatrick

The Blackbird's Nest, a tale of Saint Kevin of Ireland

Written by Jenny Schroedel / Illustrated by Doug Montross

FEAST DAY: ST. KEVIN JUNE 3

Discussion Questions

1. How old was St. Kevin when he was baptized?
2. What does the name "Kevin" mean?
3. Describe Kevin as a child. Who were Kevin's friends? How did get along with other children?
4. Why do you think St. Kevin was unable to get along with people, yet befriended the animals so easily?
5. What did the monks ask Kevin to do for Lent?
6. How many days did Christ spend in the desert?
7. What was Kevin doing when the blackbird began building her nest in his hand?
8. What did Kevin whisper as he waited and held the precious blackbird eggs in his outstretched hand? Why did he say this?
9. How many days did it take for the baby blackbirds to hatch? Do you notice the connection between Easter and the timing of the birds' hatching?
10. Why do you think St. Kevin was a changed man after the blackbird incidence?
11. Why do you think Kevin went back to build his monastery in the valley where he had spent that Lent?

Copywork

Go to the final page and read the "Historical Note". Cut an oval egg shape out of a piece of blue or green paper. Copy the *Hymn to Saint Kevin* on the egg and glue it on a sheet of bordered paper. To create the nest around the bottom of the egg, glue pieces of Easter grass, Spanish moss, sawdust, or shredded newspaper. Place in your Liturgical Year Notebook.

Parent's Help Page
The Blackbird's Nest

Observation

Look at the picture of the newborn baby blackbirds in the nest held by St. Kevin. Notice how different they are from adult birds.

Think about the colors that the illustrator chose for this story. Why do you think he used mostly green and brown? What tone or mood do the colors evoke?

Discussion Answers

1. St. Kevin was 40 days old when he was baptized.
2. The name "Kevin" means "gentle one."
3. Kevin was not gentle with other children. His friends were the animals in the forest.
4. Answers will vary. Let the child explain his answer.
5. For Lent, the monks asked Kevin to spend 40 days praying in a valley.
6. Christ spent 40 days in the desert.
7. Kevin was praying with his arms outstretched when the blackbird began building her nest in his hand.
8. Kevin whispered, "Lord, have mercy." Answers will vary; maybe he wasn't sure he would able to keep his arms up until the birds hatched.
9. It took 40 days for the baby blackbirds to hatch. The baby blackbirds hatched in time for the "great feast of Christ's Resurrection." (For a more complete understanding, read the notation found in the bird egg in the back of book.) If your child hasn't yet noticed that many things in the story take 40 days, point that out now.
10. Answers will vary.
11. Answers will vary

Enrichment Activities

1. Do an Internet or book search on blackbirds to discover various facts about them. Then write or dictate a paper showcasing your findings and adding illustrations.
2. Draw a picture of the blackbirds in Kevin's hand and put it in your Liturgical Year Notebook.
3. Create a "40 day" collage. Think of all the things in the Church calendar or in the Bible that are 40 days long. Find a large piece of paper and write "40 days" in large letters in the middle of the paper. Then draw a picture or symbol for each of the events.

Across a Dark and Wild Sea
Written and Illustrated by Don Brown

FEAST DAY: ST. COLUMCILLE, JUNE 9

Vocabulary

ignorance	scribe	bard	monastery	parchment
memorable	folio	trifle	kinsman	
scriptorium	dispatch	colony	accomplishment	

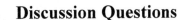

Discussion Questions

1. What "lay in the ruins" of the Roman Empire? What do you think the author means when he says that?
2. Do you think you can really eat a cake filled with letters of the alphabet? How do you think this legend came to be?
3. Where did Columcille learn how to read and write?
4. What imagery does the author use to describe monasteries?
5. What book did Finnian have that Columcille wanted a copy of? Why did Finnian refuse him?
6. What is a manuscript, and what does the word manuscript mean?
7. How did the monks make colored ink? Which color was their favorite to use for special occasions?
8. Describe what happened when Columcille finished the copy of Finnian's book?
9. Why did Columcille end up with the book?
10. How did Columcille feel after his defeat of Ireland's King Diarmait, when he was awarded his copy of the book?
11. What did Columcille decide to do?
12. How did Columcille's love of books help the world?

Copywork

To every cow her calf, to every book its copy.
—*King Diarmait to Columcille in*
Across a Dark and Wild Sea

Parent's Help Page
Across a Dark and Wild Sea

Discussion Answers

1. Knowledge and education lay in the ruins. It means that when civilization failed, learning was lost. In the struggle to survive in those difficult times, there was no time or place for knowledge and education.
2. You cannot eat a cake filled with the alphabet and learn to read. Perhaps Columcille learned so easily that people said this about him as a joke.
3. Columcille learned to read and write at a monastery where he was taught by a scribe.
4. Author Don Brown refers to monasteries as "candles of learning in a dark world."

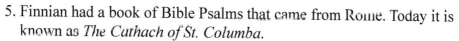

5. Finnian had a book of Bible Psalms that came from Rome. Today it is known as *The Cathach of St. Columba.*

6. In those days, a "manuscript" referred to a written copy of a book. The word means "written by hand."

7. The favorite color was red and it was used to mark special days which then became known as "red letter days."

8. Finnian found out about Columcille's copy of the book and demanded it form him, but Columcille refused. The High King was called in to make a judgment, and he said that Finnian should have the book.

9. A war began over this judgement. In the end, Columcille won the book back but many people had died.

10. Columcille felt his victory was "hollow and wrong."

11. Columcille decided to redeem himself by leaving Ireland and making a worthy life elsewhere. He founded a monastery in Scotland.

12. Answers will vary. From the monasteries, many copies of books were sent out to the world so that the light of learning might continue.

Enrichment Activities

1. Find Ireland and Scotland on a map.

2. Turn to the page that discusses and illustrates the various instruments and techniques used for early writing. On a piece of brown parchment paper (found at most printing shops) or on a brown paper bag cut and laid flat, list the tools that were used:

   • Pens—goose or swan quills
   • Ink—soot(black), oak, apples/iron (brown), mineral from Afghanistan (blue),
   • insect (red)
   • Parchment—animal skin

   Give your child a piece of coal or charred stick and have him/her copy the "Uncial Alphabet" (found in the back of the Across a Dark and Wild Sea) on a piece of parchment or brown paper bag. Find a goose feather to use as pen. Then mix some ink using crushed blackberries, cranberries, beet juice, etc. Staple parchment paper or squares of brown paper bag together into book form. Then have your child try his/her hand at using these writing tools.

3. *The Book of Kells* is the most elaborate illuminated manuscript of the Gospels to have lasted from the days of the Middle Ages. It was produced on calfskin in Ireland around the year 800 A.D. You might wish to look into doing a study of this book with your child.

   Dover Publications offers a coloring book alled *Color Your Own Book of Kells* for only $3.95. Find a copy at your local educational supply shop or online.

July

Sean Fitzpatrick

A Peek Into My Church

Written by Wendy Goody and Veronica Kelly,
Illustrated by Ginny Pruitt
Published by Whippersnapper Books, 1997.
Cover reprinted by permission of the publisher.

ORDINARY TIME

Vocabulary

sanctuary	lectionary	tabernacle
vestibule	lectern	font
reconciliation	sacristy	

Discussion Questions

1. Why do we bless ourselves with holy water whenever we enter our church?
2. What did you become through baptism?

3. Do you know the names of your godparents and the date on which you were baptized?
4. What do the flickering candles and the beautifully laid altar table remind us of?
5. When we recite the Apostle's Creed at Mass, what are we saying?
6. What does every Communion remind us of?
7. What do the bread and wine become when the priest consecrates them?
8. What other jobs does your parish priest do?
9. What are some jobs that nuns do?

Parent's Help Page
A Peek Into My Church

Observation

1. Observe the people walking to the Catholic Church. How are they dressed? Discuss why we should dress as though we are going to see a king.
2. Notice the statues inside the church. Are any of them like those that are in your church? Statues serve to remind us of those who led exemplary lives of holiness.
3. Observe the collages of different Catholic communities at the end of the book. Discuss them.
4. Look over and discuss the various items of clothing a priest wears.
5. Discuss the Picture Dictionary at the back of the book.

Discussion Answers

1. Blessing ourselves with holy water reminds us of our Christian baptism.
2. Your baptism made you a member of the Catholic Church.
3. Give your child the names of his/her godparents and the date of his/her baptism.
4. The candles and altar table remind us of how we set a pretty table when we have guests come to eat at our house.
5. When we say the Apostle's Creed, we are declaring what we believe in as Catholics.
6. Every Communion reminds us of the Last Supper. (Here parents might want to discuss how Communion is known as the "Sacrifice of the Mass," and it is then that Jesus' Passion and Death on the Cross is re-presented.)
7. The bread and wine become the Body and Blood of Jesus.

8. Priests have many other jobs such as celebrating Mass, visiting the sick, praying for us, counseling us, teaching us, witnessing marriages, and baptizing babies.
9. Nuns do jobs such as teaching in schools and working in hospitals and communities.

Enrichment Activities

1. On a sheet of paper, draw (or have your child draw) the layout of your parish church. Clip the paper to a clipboard. Take your child to our parish church one day during the week and have your child fill in the outline by identifying the location of the pews, the baptismal font, the altar, sanctuary, etc.
2. Have a picture of your child's baptism on hand to show him/her.
3. Make a proper Sign of the Cross.
4. Go to Catholic Heritage Curricula's website to view links where you can get an insider's view on vocations: http://www.catholichomeschooling.com/curr/vocations.htm.

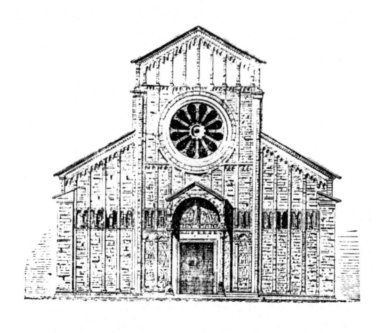

The Legend of Saint Christopher

Written by Margaret Hodges/ Illustrated by Richard Jesse Watson
Published by Eerdmans, 2002. Cover reprinted by permission of the publisher.

Christopher: The Holy Giant

Written and Illustrated by Tomie dePaola

FEAST DAY: ST. CHRISTOPHER, JULY 25

Discussion Questions

1. Why did both characters go in search of a king and the devil?
2. What made the devil run away?
3. Whom do Offero and Reprobus seek out next in their search for Christ?
4. Where does the hermit tell them they will find Christ?
5. How many times does the voice of the child call before appearing? Why do you think he doesn't show himself the first two times?

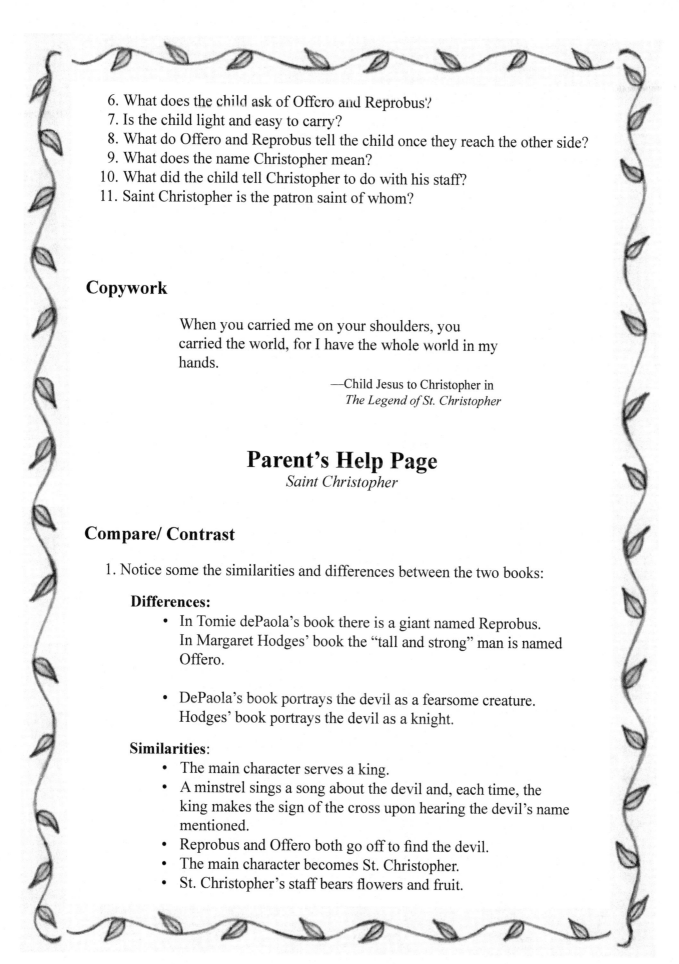

6. What does the child ask of Offero and Reprobus?
7. Is the child light and easy to carry?
8. What do Offero and Reprobus tell the child once they reach the other side?
9. What does the name Christopher mean?
10. What did the child tell Christopher to do with his staff?
11. Saint Christopher is the patron saint of whom?

Copywork

When you carried me on your shoulders, you carried the world, for I have the whole world in my hands.

—Child Jesus to Christopher in
The Legend of St. Christopher

Parent's Help Page
Saint Christopher

Compare/ Contrast

1. Notice some the similarities and differences between the two books:

Differences:

- In Tomie dePaola's book there is a giant named Reprobus. In Margaret Hodges' book the "tall and strong" man is named Offero.

- DePaola's book portrays the devil as a fearsome creature. Hodges' book portrays the devil as a knight.

Similarities:

- The main character serves a king.
- A minstrel sings a song about the devil and, each time, the king makes the sign of the cross upon hearing the devil's name mentioned.
- Reprobus and Offero both go off to find the devil.
- The main character becomes St. Christopher.
- St. Christopher's staff bears flowers and fruit.

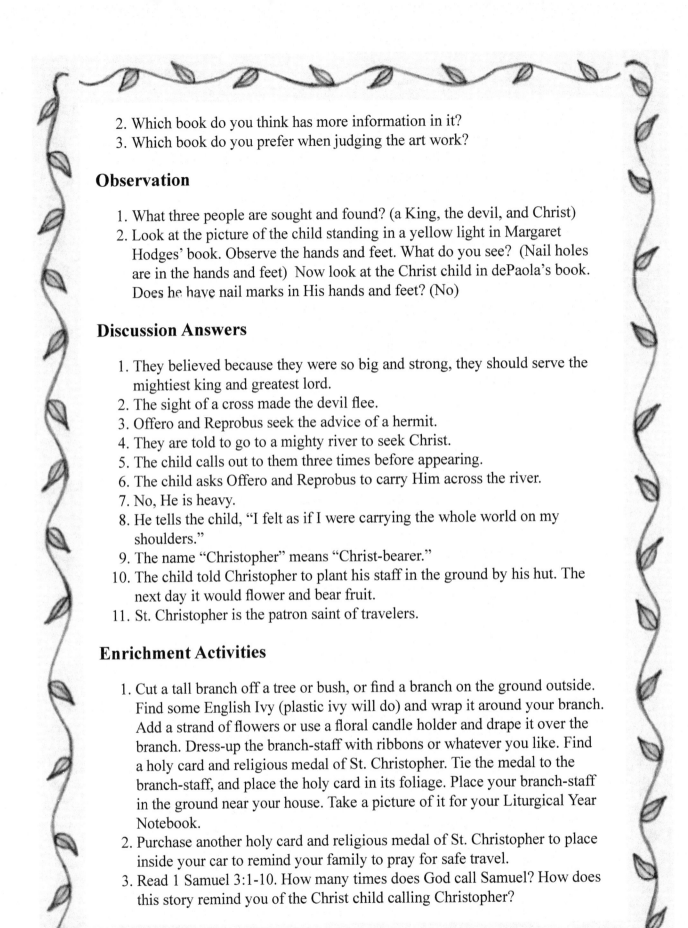

2. Which book do you think has more information in it?
3. Which book do you prefer when judging the art work?

Observation

1. What three people are sought and found? (a King, the devil, and Christ)
2. Look at the picture of the child standing in a yellow light in Margaret Hodges' book. Observe the hands and feet. What do you see? (Nail holes are in the hands and feet) Now look at the Christ child in dePaola's book. Does he have nail marks in His hands and feet? (No)

Discussion Answers

1. They believed because they were so big and strong, they should serve the mightiest king and greatest lord.
2. The sight of a cross made the devil flee.
3. Offero and Reprobus seek the advice of a hermit.
4. They are told to go to a mighty river to seek Christ.
5. The child calls out to them three times before appearing.
6. The child asks Offero and Reprobus to carry Him across the river.
7. No, He is heavy.
8. He tells the child, "I felt as if I were carrying the whole world on my shoulders."
9. The name "Christopher" means "Christ-bearer."
10. The child told Christopher to plant his staff in the ground by his hut. The next day it would flower and bear fruit.
11. St. Christopher is the patron saint of travelers.

Enrichment Activities

1. Cut a tall branch off a tree or bush, or find a branch on the ground outside. Find some English Ivy (plastic ivy will do) and wrap it around your branch. Add a strand of flowers or use a floral candle holder and drape it over the branch. Dress-up the branch-staff with ribbons or whatever you like. Find a holy card and religious medal of St. Christopher. Tie the medal to the branch-staff, and place the holy card in its foliage. Place your branch-staff in the ground near your house. Take a picture of it for your Liturgical Year Notebook.
2. Purchase another holy card and religious medal of St. Christopher to place inside your car to remind your family to pray for safe travel.
3. Read 1 Samuel 3:1-10. How many times does God call Samuel? How does this story remind you of the Christ child calling Christopher?

August

Sean Fitzpatrick

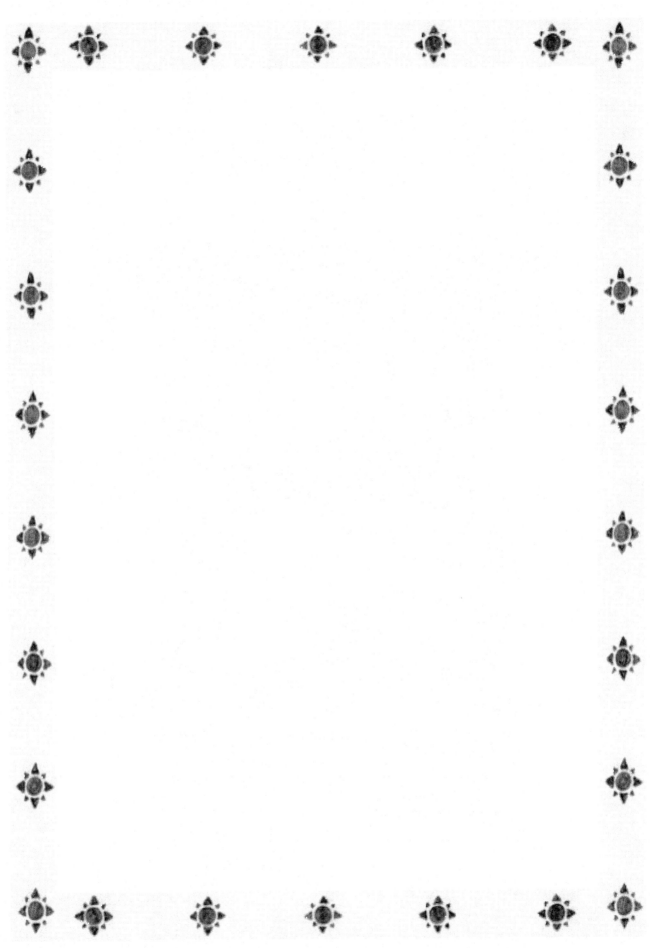

Juanita and Our Lady of the Angels
Written and Illustrated by Elizabeth Loch
Published by Precious Life Books, Inc, 2001.
Cover reprinted by permission of the publisher.

FEAST DAY: AUGUST 2, OUR LADY OF THE ANGELS

Vocabulary

segregation   mestizos   hammock   imagination   encase
investigate   consecration   parishioners   tabernacle   territory
replica   pilgrim   alleviate   reliquary   tribute
mural   pilgrimage   shrine   disciple   granite
coronation   patroness   mantle

Discussion

1 What did Juanita think the rock looked like?
2. Why did Juanita bring the rock to the priest?
3. Where did the priest hide the rock? Why do you think he hid it there?
4. Who did Juanita think was bringing the doll back to the stream?
5. Read the copywork assignment supplied for this study. Who else did the Virgin Mary say these words to?
6. What does the Blessed Mother expect her children to do?

Copywork

I am your merciful Mother. Here I will hear your weeping and your sorrows, and alleviate all your multiple sufferings, necessities and misfortunes. And here I will give my help and my protection to the people.

—Virgin Mary to Juan Diego in Guadalupe, Mexico, in 1531

Parent's Help Page
Juanita and Our Lady of the Angels

Discussion Answers

1. Juanita thought the rock looked like a doll.
2. Juanita brought the rock to the priest because it kept disappearing from her house and reappearing by the stream.
3. The priest hid the rock in the tabernacle.
4. Juanita thought the angels were bringing the doll back.
5. The Virgin Mary said these words to the Indian in Guadalupe, Juan Diego.
6. The Blessed Mother expects her children to make a pilgrimage to one of her shrines each year.

Enrichment Activities

1. Study the map of Costa Rica located in front of the book and then label the country on your world map (See Map Appendix.).

2. Use the outline map of Costa Rice provided in the Appendix. Draw a picture of the little Marian statue from this story on it. Then place it in your Liturgical Year Notebook. Or print out a map of Costa Rica that includes landforms or cities and place a sticker on it Where the shrine of Our Lady of the Angels is located.

3. Make a Marian Shrine:

   — **Materials needed:**

   > small shoe box
   > plastic/silk flowers
   > moss and/or greenery
   > small rock
   > foil
   > black paint
   > white paint pen
   > plastic baby found in King Cakes or party stores
   > other decorative accessories
   > cement glue
   > rosary
   > mosaic tile chips

   — **Directions:**

   Clean a small rock and paint it black. While the rock is drying, wrap the shoe box in foil and decorate with flowers and foliage. Put it in a standing position. When rock is dry, use a white paint pen to draw Mary's face on top of rock. An alternative is to simply use a holy card of the Blessed Mother and prop it against the rock. Use cement glue to glue the plastic baby in place on the rock as though Mary is cradling Baby Jesus. Place Marian rock image in the center of the decorated shrine. Place mosaic tile chips at her feet and twine the rosary around the shrine.

4. Is there a Marian shrine near you? Plan a field trip to the shrine. Prepare in advance to make the trip a mini-pilgrimage. Discuss the difference between a field trip and a pilgrimage.

Brother Bartholomew and the Apple Grove
Written by Jan Cheripko/ Illustrated by Kestutis Kasparavicius
Published by Boyds Mills Press, 2004.
Cover reprinted by permission of the publisher

ORDINARY TIME: HARVEST

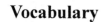

Vocabulary

rheumatism	rickety	appall	wary
drench	catapult	majestic	collapse

Discussion

1. What did Brother Bartholomew always say when the other monks worried about the deer eating the apples?
2. How did Brother Stephen feel when he visited Brother Bartholomew on his deathbed? Why?
3. What did Brother Bartholomew tell Brother Stephen?
4. How did Brother Stephen feel when he left Brother Bartholomew's deathbed? Why?
5. What is the final task Brother Stephen does to keep the deer out of the apple grove?
6. What does Brother Stephen do to the deer injured by the barbed wire? Why?
7. Does Brother Stephen change? In what way does he change?
8. What does Brother Stephen tell the young monk, Brother Francis, who has come to the monastery?

Copywork

God will provide. He always does.
—words of Brother Bartholomew in
Brother Bartholomew and the Apple Grove

Pride goeth before destruction, and a haughty spirit before a fall. Better it is to be of a humble spirit with the lowly, than to divide the spoil with the proud.
—Prov. 16:18-19).

Parent's Help Page
Brother Bartholomew and the Apple Grove

Observation

1. What were some of the tasks the monk performed? (Tend the sheep, harvest the vegetables and fruit, spin wool into clothing, make jams and jellies, and cook applesauce.)

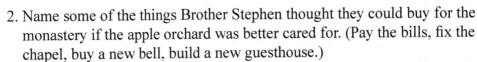

2. Name some of the things Brother Stephen thought they could buy for the monastery if the apple orchard was better cared for. (Pay the bills, fix the chapel, buy a new bell, build a new guesthouse.)
3. When Brother Stephen visits Brother Bartholomew on his deathbed, how can you tell that he is, at first, ashamed and guilty? (You can tell he is guilty because he stares at the floor and, when he does look at his brother monk, he quickly turns away.) How can you tell he is joyful after Brother Bartholomew forgives him? ("His heart leapt with with joy.")
4. Compare Brother Bartholomew and Brother Stephen. Do you think it's possible Brother Bartholomew was like Brother Stephen when he was a young monk? Explain your answer.

Discussion Answers

1. Brother Bartholomew would always say, "God will provide. He always does."
2. Brother Stephen felt ashamed and guilty when he visited Brother Bartholomew because he had wished Brother Bartholomew would die so that he could take charge of the apple orchard.
3. Brother Bartholomew told Brother Stephen that he forgave him and told him: "Tend my apples."
4. Brother Stephen was full of joy because Brother Bartholomew had entrusted the apple grove to him.
5. Brother Stephen puts a roll of barbed wire across the top of the fence to keep the deer out.
6. Brother Stephen kneels beside the deer and weeps. He cries because he realizes that he was willing to destroy another of God's creation our of pride—he knows that he has been a fool.
7. Yes, Brother Stephen changes.
8. Brother Stephen tells the new monk the same words the Brother Bartholomew told him: "God will provide. He always does."

Enrichment Activity

Meditate on Brother Stephen's behavior in this book. Ask yourself:
Where is my heart? Where does God want it to be? What is my treasure? Where does God want it to be? Then draw a beautiful treasure chest. Write on it the treasure of your heart, and place your drawing in your Liturgical Year Notebook.

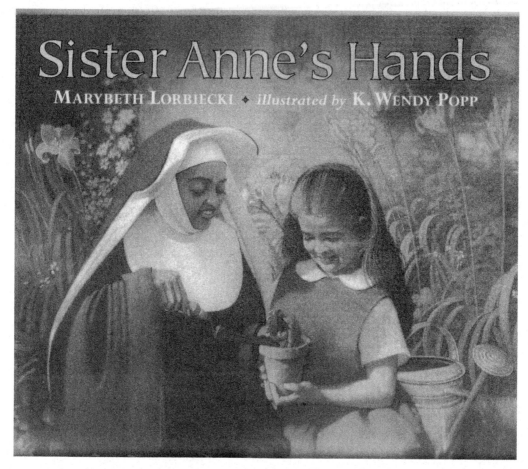

Sister Anne's Hands

Written by Marybeth Lorbiecki/ Illustrated by K. Wendy Popp
Published by Penguin Books for Young Readers, 2000.
Cover reprinted by permission of the publisher.

ORDINARY TIME: GARDENING

Vocabulary

Plaster   slunk   minister   transfer

Discussion Questions

1. What did Sister Anne say had kissed Anna's face where her freckles were?
2. Did the children like their new teacher? Why?
3. How did Sister Anne make learning fun?

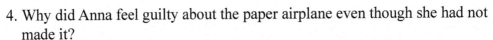

4. Why did Anna feel guilty about the paper airplane even though she had not made it?
5. Why do you think Sister Anne put pictures on the board?
6. Why do you think some parents pulled their children out of Sister Anne's classroom?
7. Choose one of the following historical figures and find out who he or she was: Phillis Wheatley, Matthew Henson, Sojourner Truth, Dr. Martin Luther King.
8. What was Sister Anne trying to teach the children?

Copywork

I'd rather open my door enough to let everyone in
than risk slamming it shut on God's big toe.
—words of Sister Anne in *Sister Anne's Hands*

Parent's Help Page
Sister Anne's Hands

Observation

Before reading this story with your child, ask him/her what he/she thinks this book might be about.

Discussion Answers

1. Angels.
2. Yes.
3. She made learning fun by telling jokes and by having the children count buttons on clothes, pencils in desk, teeth in heads, etc. (Allow your child to look at the pictures and add things he sees the children doing)
4. Anna felt guilty because the class had giggled and thought the rhyme was funny. Was it?
5. She wanted to teach the children the cruelty that humans can inflect on one another.
6. They were upset that their children had seen the ugly pictures and been told some harsh realities.
7. Help your child research one of these famous African American personalities.

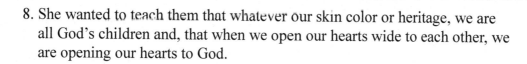

8. She wanted to teach them that whatever our skin color or heritage, we are all God's children and, that when we open our hearts wide to each other, we are opening our hearts to God.

Enrichment Activity

Mosaic Hand Print Collage
1. Give your child pencils, markers, and a sheet of white construction paper or card stock.
2. Have him trace his hands on the paper. He can copy the left hand over the right print and then trace his hands at various angles on the paper.
3. Next, let him decorate and color his hands like Anna did at the end of the book.
4. Allow him to do his copywork on the mosaic print if he wants.
5. Place the hand print in your Liturgical Year Notebook.

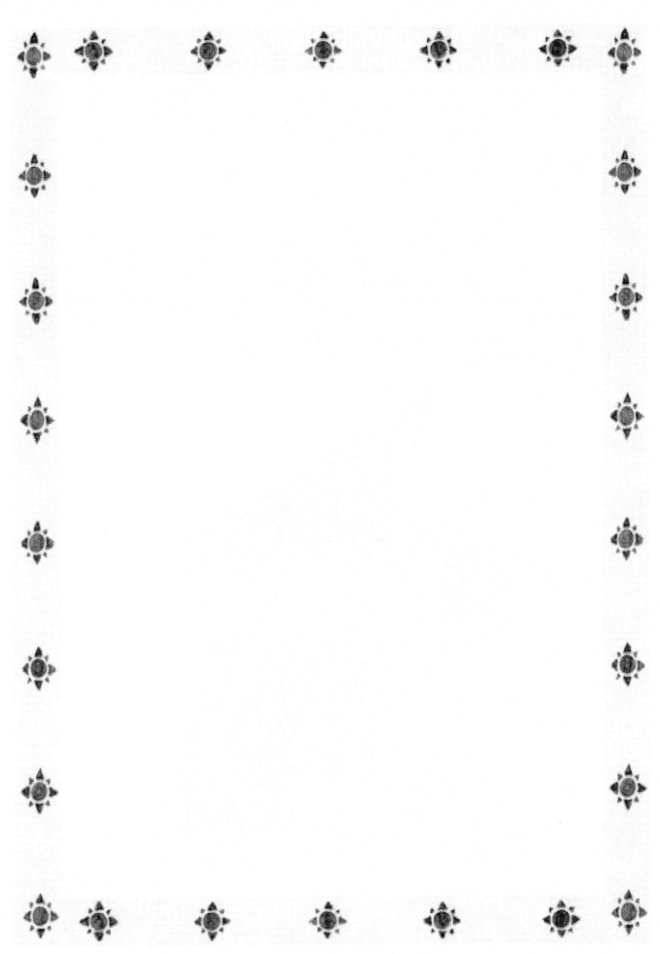

September

Sean Fitzpatrick

Mother Teresa
Written and Illustrated by Demi

FEAST DAY: SEPTEMBER 5

Vocabulary

vivid	shantytown	vow	inoculate	provisions
cyclone	slum	decisive	malnutrition	self-sufficient
devastation	destitute	famine	ferocious	rehabilitate
humanitarian	ethnic	humility	inspiration	supplement
galvanizer	aspirant	postulant	theology	intense

Discussion Questions

1. What was Mother Teresa's real name?
2. As a school girl, what did Mother Teresa want to become?
3. How old was Mother Teresa when she felt called to the religious life?
4. Which saint did Mother Teresa chose to be named after?
5. Calcutta's worst slum was named Moti Jheel. What does this phrase mean?
6. What was September 10, 1946, known as and why?
7. What was the first thing Mother Teresa did when she walked into Moti Jheel? Why do you think she did that first?
8. When was Mother Teresa's new congregation approved, and what was its name?
9. What were the vows the nuns took in this new order?
10. What prayer inspired Mother Teresa? Why do you think she liked it so much?

Copywork

The more you give away, the more you receive.
—Mother Teresa of Calcutta

It is not how much we do
But how much love
We put in the doing
That makes our offering
Something beautiful for God.
—Mother Teresa of Calcutta

Parent's Help Page
Mother Teresa

Observation

Find Macedonia on a map. Mother Teresa was born and raised here.
Find Ireland on the map. Mother Teresa went here to join the Sisters of Loreto.
Find Calcutta on the map. This is where Mother Teresa spent the rest of her life.

Remember the Seven Corporal Works of Mercy discussed in *The Little Match Girl* study? Mother Teresa lived out these works of mercy, showing us how to serve others with Christ as our inspiration and motivation. Review them.

Study Demi's detailed pictures with your children so you can appreciate just how much there is to see, learn, and understand about a way of life truly foreign to Americans.

Discussion Answers

1. Mother Teresa's given name was Agnes Gonxha Bojaxhiu.
2. Mother Teresa wanted to become a missionary.
3. Mother Teresa was 12 years old when she felt called to the religious life.
4. Mother Teresa chose to be named after St. Teresa of Lisieux, the Little Flower.
5. Moti Jheel means "Pearl Lake."
6. September 10, 1946, became known as Inspiration Day because it was on this day that Mother Teresa was "inspired" to live among the "poorest of the poor" and help them.
7. The first thing Mother Teresa did in Moti Jheel was to gather children around her and begin a "school" under a tree.
8. Mother Teresa's new congregation was approved in 1950; it was called the Missionaries of Charity.
9. The nuns took vows of poverty, chastity, obedience, and service to the poorest of the poor.
10. The *Anima Christe* of St. Ignatius of Loyola inspired Mother Teresa.

Enrichment Activities

1. One can easily learn the lovely *Anima Christe* prayer by listening to it sung by the beautiful voice of Donna Cori Gibson at her website: www.donnacorigibson.com
2. How can you be like Mother Teresa in your own home? Remember that she always looked to St. Therese of Lisieux, the Little Flower, as her example; doing only small things with great love.
3. Begin to do within your own home with your own family as Mother Teresa instructed us:

> We serve Jesus in [our home], we nurse Him, feed Him, clothe Him, visit Him, and comfort Him in [our home]. All we do—our prayer, our work, our suffering—is for Jesus. Our life has no other reason or motivation.
> —Mother Teresa of Calcutta

> Never let anyone come to you without coming away better and happier. Everyone should see goodness in your face, in your eyes, in your smile.
> —Mother Teresa of Calcutta

4. Demi supplies a host of memorial days in the life of Mother Teresa. Create a timeline sheet to go in your Liturgical Year Notebook using the timeline provided in *Mother Teresa*.

Sean Fitzpatrick

Peter Claver

~ Patron Saint of Slaves ~
Written by Julia Durango / Illustrated by Rebecca Garcia-Franco

FEAST DAY: SEPTEMBER 9

Vocabulary

cleanse   bandage   plantation   plague   chorus   canonize

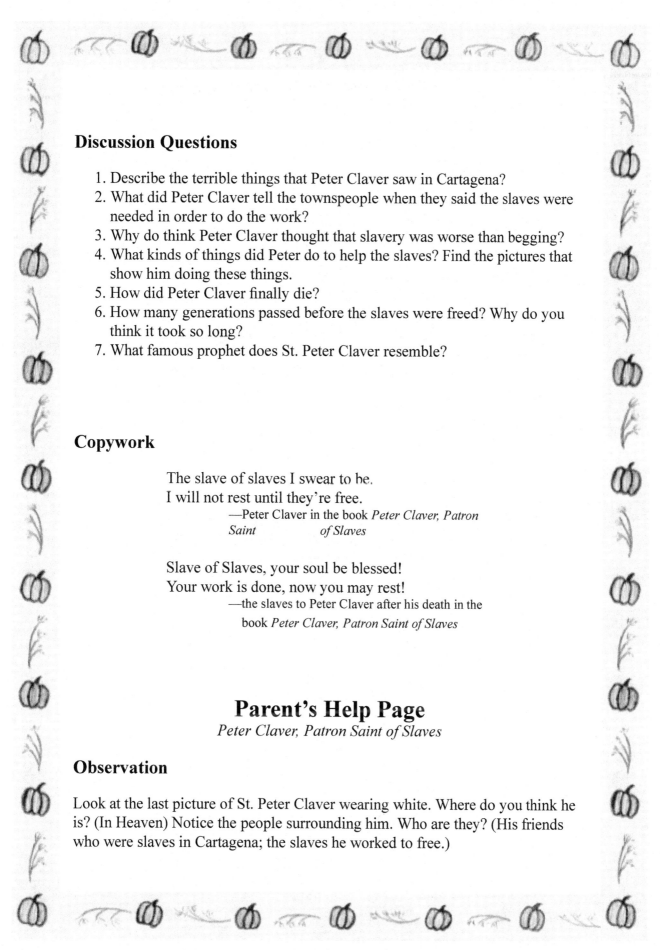

Discussion Questions

1. Describe the terrible things that Peter Claver saw in Cartagena?
2. What did Peter Claver tell the townspeople when they said the slaves were needed in order to do the work?
3. Why do think Peter Claver thought that slavery was worse than begging?
4. What kinds of things did Peter do to help the slaves? Find the pictures that show him doing these things.
5. How did Peter Claver finally die?
6. How many generations passed before the slaves were freed? Why do you think it took so long?
7. What famous prophet does St. Peter Claver resemble?

Copywork

The slave of slaves I swear to be.
I will not rest until they're free.
   —Peter Claver in the book *Peter Claver, Patron Saint   of Slaves*

Slave of Slaves, your soul be blessed!
Your work is done, now you may rest!
   —the slaves to Peter Claver after his death in the book *Peter Claver, Patron Saint of Slaves*

Parent's Help Page
Peter Claver, Patron Saint of Slaves

Observation

Look at the last picture of St. Peter Claver wearing white. Where do you think he is? (In Heaven) Notice the people surrounding him. Who are they? (His friends who were slaves in Cartagena; the slaves he worked to free.)

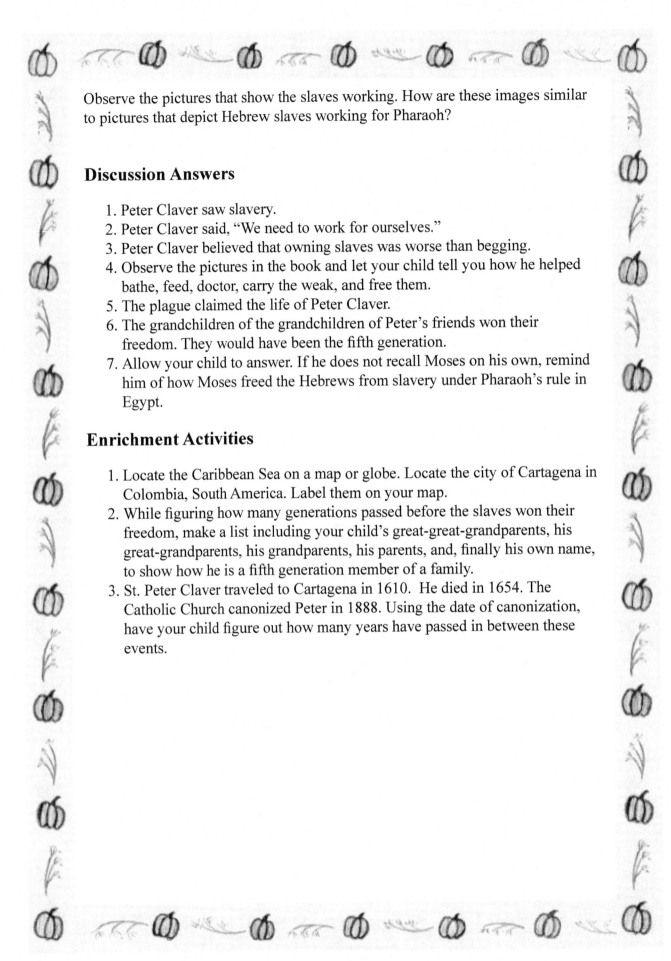

Observe the pictures that show the slaves working. How are these images similar to pictures that depict Hebrew slaves working for Pharaoh?

Discussion Answers

1. Peter Claver saw slavery.
2. Peter Claver said, "We need to work for ourselves."
3. Peter Claver believed that owning slaves was worse than begging.
4. Observe the pictures in the book and let your child tell you how he helped bathe, feed, doctor, carry the weak, and free them.
5. The plague claimed the life of Peter Claver.
6. The grandchildren of the grandchildren of Peter's friends won their freedom. They would have been the fifth generation.
7. Allow your child to answer. If he does not recall Moses on his own, remind him of how Moses freed the Hebrews from slavery under Pharaoh's rule in Egypt.

Enrichment Activities

1. Locate the Caribbean Sea on a map or globe. Locate the city of Cartagena in Colombia, South America. Label them on your map.
2. While figuring how many generations passed before the slaves won their freedom, make a list including your child's great-great-grandparents, his great-grandparents, his grandparents, his parents, and, finally his own name, to show how he is a fifth generation member of a family.
3. St. Peter Claver traveled to Cartagena in 1610. He died in 1654. The Catholic Church canonized Peter in 1888. Using the date of canonization, have your child figure out how many years have passed in between these events.

Sean Fitzpatrick

The Tale of Three Trees
Retold by Angela Elwell Hunt / Illustrated by Tim Jonke

FEAST DAY: TRIUMPH OF THE CROSS, SEPTEMBER 14

Vocabulary

startle   yank   flinch   jeer   harsh

Discussion Questions

1. What did the first little tree wish to be?
2. What did the second little tree wish to be?
3. What did the third little tree wish to be?
4. What did the first little tree become?
5. What did the second little tree become?
6. What did the third little tree become?
7. Do you think any of them became what they had wished to be? Explain.
8. What treasure did the first little tree end up holding?
9. What king did the second little tree end up carrying?
10. What was the third tree's destiny and how did people think of God because of her?
11. What can we learn about our own relationship with God from this story?

Copywork

I want to grow so tall that when people stop to look
at me they will raise their eyes to heaven and think
of God.

—the third tree's wish in
The Tale of Three Trees

Parent's Help Page
Tale of Three Trees

Observation

1. Parents: Take a moment to explain to your child that a *cross* is without the body of Christ. A *crucifix* is a cross with the corpse of Christ upon it.
2. Walk through your house and look at any crosses/crucifixes that are on the walls or that are in pictures. As much as they are the same, how are they different?
3. If you have a computer, go online and type in "cross images." With a parent's guidance, search for different cross images. Visit a church or cemetery to observe the different designs found on crosses.

4. Visit this webpage: http://www.promiseofgod.com/dogwood/. Or, do a search for "The Legend of the Dogwood Tree" to read another famous story of a tree that served as a cross for Our Lord. Dogwood trees bloom before, on, or shortly after Easter Sunday. Be on the lookout for a dogwood tree and remember that these blossoms commemorate the Passion of Our Lord:

> The once strong tree is now gnarled and withered,
> The blossoms are in the form of a cross,
> Each petal bears a rusty nail mark and a blood-stained trace,
> The flower's center represents the crown of thorns,
> And the white flower blushes from shame.

> —Source unknown

Discussion Answers

1. The first little tree wished to be a beautiful treasure chest.
2. The second little tree wished to be a strong sailing ship.
3. The third little tree wished to be the tallest tree in the world and have people look to heaven and think of God when they looked at her.
4. The first little tree became a feed box for animals.
5. The second little tree became a simple fishing boat.
6. The third little tree became beams in a lumberyard.
7. None of them turned out to be what he/she had wished for.
8. The first little tree ended up holding the greatest treasure in the world, our Lord Jesus Christ.
9. The second little tree ended up carrying the King of heaven and Earth.
10. The third little tree's destiny was to become the cross that Jesus was crucified upon. Yet, even over 2,000 years later, the cross is the symbol of Jesus' saving grace—and people all over the world think of God when they see it.
11. Answers will vary. Let your child ponder this and talk about it with you.

Enrichment Activity

Draw a collage of the various crosses you have found. Or, take pictures and make a collage with them. Be sure to add you collage to your Liturgical Year Notebook.

St. Jerome and the Lion
Retold by Margaret Hodges/ Illustrated by Barry Moser

FEAST DAY: SEPTEMBER 30

Vocabulary

plow	suspicious	translate	harness	caravan
sow	vigil	prowl	guilty	innocent

Discussion Questions

1. Whom is St. Jerome the patron saint of ?
2. What did St. Jerome build in Bethlehem?
3. Into what language did St. Jerome translate the Bible? Why?
4. Why do you think St. Jerome did not run away in fear from the lion?

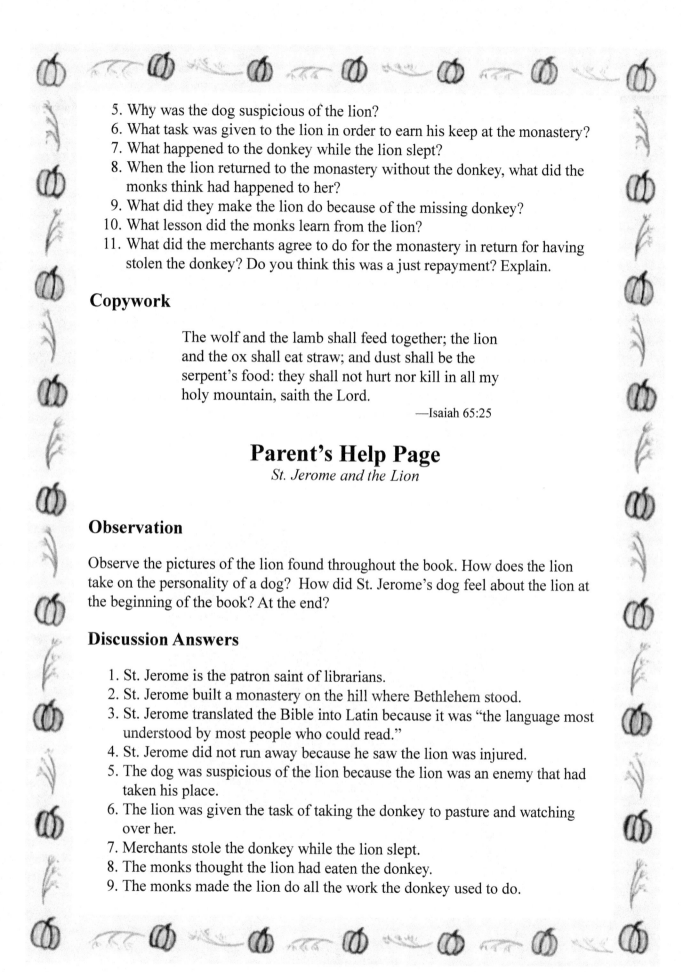

5. Why was the dog suspicious of the lion?
6. What task was given to the lion in order to earn his keep at the monastery?
7. What happened to the donkey while the lion slept?
8. When the lion returned to the monastery without the donkey, what did the monks think had happened to her?
9. What did they make the lion do because of the missing donkey?
10. What lesson did the monks learn from the lion?
11. What did the merchants agree to do for the monastery in return for having stolen the donkey? Do you think this was a just repayment? Explain.

Copywork

The wolf and the lamb shall feed together; the lion and the ox shall eat straw; and dust shall be the serpent's food: they shall not hurt nor kill in all my holy mountain, saith the Lord.

—Isaiah 65:25

Parent's Help Page
St. Jerome and the Lion

Observation

Observe the pictures of the lion found throughout the book. How does the lion take on the personality of a dog? How did St. Jerome's dog feel about the lion at the beginning of the book? At the end?

Discussion Answers

1. St. Jerome is the patron saint of librarians.
2. St. Jerome built a monastery on the hill where Bethlehem stood.
3. St. Jerome translated the Bible into Latin because it was "the language most understood by most people who could read."
4. St. Jerome did not run away because he saw the lion was injured.
5. The dog was suspicious of the lion because the lion was an enemy that had taken his place.
6. The lion was given the task of taking the donkey to pasture and watching over her.
7. Merchants stole the donkey while the lion slept.
8. The monks thought the lion had eaten the donkey.
9. The monks made the lion do all the work the donkey used to do.

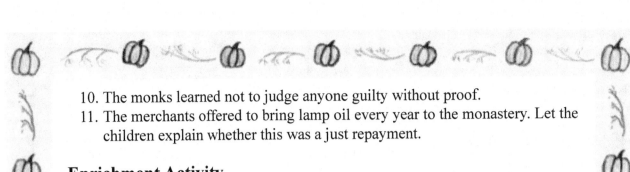

10. The monks learned not to judge anyone guilty without proof.
11. The merchants offered to bring lamp oil every year to the monastery. Let the children explain whether this was a just repayment.

Enrichment Activity

1. Compile a list of some of the tasks the monks had to do at the monastery. Compare and contrast these tasks to things that you do at home. The child may mention any of the following and then name things happen at his house that are similar: cook soup, bake bread, tend grape vines and olive trees, plow the fields, sow the seeds, gather the harvest, shear the sheep, collect firewood, translate books. Take a large sheet of drawing paper and fold it in half. On one side illustrate the things that the monks had to do, and on the other side then illustrate the things that you do. Place this is your Liturgical Year Notebook.
2. Investigate the life of St. Jerome, including information about his translation of the Bible. His version is called the *Vulgate*.
3. Draw a picture of St. Jerome and his lion.

October

Sean Fitzpatrick

Angel in the Waters
Written by Regina Doman/ Illustrated by Ben Hatke
Published by Sophia Institute Press, 2004.
Cover reprinted by permission of the publisher.

RESPECT LIFE MONTH

Discussion Questions

1. Who is with the new baby?
2. Where does the angel tell the baby he is?
3. What does the angel tell the baby he felt pushing on him?
4. Why does the baby miss his angel after he is born?
5. How will the baby know when his angel is near?
6. At the book's end, the angel is talking about another world. What is it called?
7. When can you tell that your angel is near you?

Parent's Help Page

Angel in the Waters

Observation

Look at the first picture. Does this picture remind you of the story of creation in Genesis when God created the world? How? What is it showing instead?

Discussion Answers

1. His angel.
2. In his Mother.
3. The world outside his mother's womb.
4. The baby is used to talking with his angel while in the waters. Now everything is different and strange.
5. He will know his angel is near when he is quiet.
6. Heaven.
7. Answers will vary.

Activities:

1. Your guardian angel was your first friend. He/She deserves a name. Can you think of an appropriate name for him/her? Perhaps Michael or Angelica, Gabriel or Celeste. Think of a name for your guardian angel. He/She will love it!

2. Spiritually adopt a baby who is in need of your prayers. See the sample *Spiritual Adoption Card* (right). See a full size card that may be photocopied in the Appendix. Laminate your card if you can and keep it in a safe place.

3. Pray the Guardian Angel Prayer every night in the silence of your room. Be quiet and do not fear. Your guardian angel is always there.

Spiritual Adoption Card

Baby's Name

_____

I will pray for nine months

from _____ (month)

until _____ (month).

My Guardian Dear

Written and Illustrated by Miriam Lademan & Susan Brindle
Published by Precious Life Books, Inc, 1996.
Cover reprinted by permission of the publisher.

FEAST DAY: GUARDIAN ANGELS, OCTOBER 2

Vocabulary

accompany | protrude | predicament | reproach
peninsula | absorb | awkward | consciousness
preoccupied | stray | devotion | guardian
perfection | emphatically | sublime | venture
eternity | companion | frail | inexpressibly
caress | redemption | resplendent | persecutor
elate | sentiment | martyr | repentance

Discussion Questions

1. Why did Angela become wander too far?
2. Describe what Francis and Mary witnessed at the pier.
3. What did Angela feel while she was in the water, and what did she see on the shore?
4. Whom did she think had saved her? Why did she think that?
5. Why did Angela feel compelled to learn more about her guardian angel?
6. Who had Angela been named after?
7. What was the name of the angel name that visited Angela and Mary?
8. When do we celebrate the Feast of the Guardian Angels?
9. What saints did the angel Gloriel show the children?

Copywork

Traditional Guardian Angel Prayer

Angel of God, my guardian dear,
To whom God's Love commits me here,
Ever this day be at my side
To light and guard, to rule and guide.
Amen.

Parent's Help Page
My Guardian Dear

Observation

1. Locate Chesapeake Bay on a map. Label it on the world or United States map provided in the Appendix.
2. Have you ever seen your guardian angel? Do you believe your guardian angel has ever saved your life? Have you shared your experience with anyone? Why not share it now with your children and let them share their experiences.

3. Observe the picture of the children and Gloriel inside the church. Why are there so many angels around the altar? Suggest that your child keep this picture in his mind the next time he is at Mass so he will realize that, when the priest elevates the holy Eucharist, all the angels in Heaven bow down to worship Him.
4. Find a Miraculous Medal and examine it closely. What are the words that surround the image of the Blessed Mother?

Discussion Answers

1. Angela became so absorbed in search for sea shells that she wandered too far.
2. The child should describe Francis and Mary seeing Angela fall into the water.
3. Angela felt someone pull her from the water and she saw a loving face.
4. She believed it was her guardian angel because there was no person there after she was saved. She felt such great love. The child may have other answers.
5. Answers may vary.
6. Angela was named after the holy angels.
7. The angel's name was Gloriel.
8. Feast of the Guardian Angels is on October 2.
9. Gloriel showed the children St. Dominic Savio, St. Germaine, St. Catherine Laboure, St. Don Bosco, St. Theodosius, and St. Rose of Lima. Take time to discuss each one and his/her relationship with his/her angel.

Enrichment Activities

1. Guardian Angels should never be without a name. Have you named yours? If you didn't name your Guardian Angel when studying the book *Angel in the Waters*, do so now. Here are a few suggestions for "angelic names."
   Angelica   Gloria   Hark   Pearl
2. Encourage your child to narrate one of the stories from the book about a saint and his/her angel.
3. Older children might learn the hierarchies of the angels as listed below.

First Hierarchy	Second Hierarchy	Third Hierarchy
Seraphim	Dominions	Principalities
Cherubim	Virtues	Archangels
Thrones	Powers	Angels

4. Draw a picture of the angels around the altar at Mass. Color it and place it in your Liturgical Year Notebook.

The Good Man of Assisi
Written by Mary Joslin/ Illustrated by Alison Wisenfeld

FEAST DAY: OCTOBER 4

Vocabulary

friar   stigmata   console   eternal   despair   pardon

Discussion Questions

1. Describe the childhood of Francis. Do you think he had a good childhood?
2. What did Francis long to be?
3. Why did he go back home the second time?
4. What made Francis change?
5. How did he change?
6. What were the people who decided to join St. Francis and live like he did called?
7. What did Francis love?
8. What Christmas tradition did St. Francis begin?
9. How was St. Francis like Christ?
10. How did St. Francis leave this world?
11. Why do you think he died gladly?

Copywork

Find the Peace Prayer of St. Francis in Appendix A. Did you know that St. Francis did not write this peace poem? This poem is believed to have been written during World War I by a Catholic priest. It is often associated with St. Francis because of his gentle nature and peaceful teachings.

Parent's Help Page
The Good Man of Assisi

Observation

Go through the book with your child. Look carefully at the pictures. See if you can spot St. Francis in each picture. Ask your child for his thoughts and feelings concerning the pictures.

Discussion Answers

1. Let the child describe. Yes, he did have a good childhood.
2. Francis longed to be a knight.
3. He had a dream in which he was told to go home and serve a different lord.
4. Francis kept remembering how Jesus had treated others in this world.
5. Francis changed by giving away everything he owned, leaving his home, and helping other people.
6. Those people were called friars.
7. Francis loved everything in the world that God had made—even worms.
8. St. Francis began the tradition of the live nativity scene, called the creche.
9. St. Francis was given the wounds of Christ, the stigmata.
10. St. Francis left this world poor and weak.
11. He died gladly because he knew he would be closer to God.

Enrichment Activity

Take out your copywork, and place it on colored cardstock or construction paper. Find pictures of various animals in magazines, cut them out, and glue them around the copywork to create a frame. While searching for pictures, discuss how each of us can bring peace to the world. Put your framed Prayer of St. Francis in your Liturgical Year Notebook.

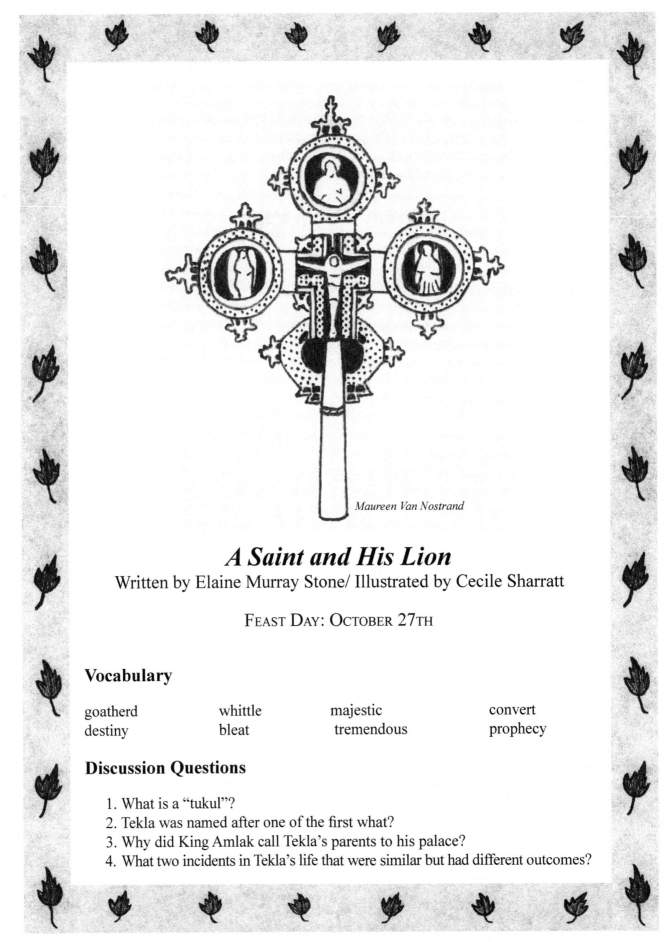

Maureen Van Nostrand

A Saint and His Lion
Written by Elaine Murray Stone/ Illustrated by Cecile Sharratt

Feast Day: October 27th

Vocabulary

goatherd	whittle	majestic	convert
destiny	bleat	tremendous	prophecy

Discussion Questions

1. What is a "tukul"?
2. Tekla was named after one of the first what?
3. Why did King Amlak call Tekla's parents to his palace?
4. What two incidents in Tekla's life that were similar but had different outcomes?

5. What is the Ethiopian word for "lion"?
6. Why did Tekla leave the monastery after taking his vows as a priest?
7. Why didn't Tekla get a stick to make another crutch?
8. Why didn't the lion attack him?
9. Were Tekla's parents proud of him? Explain why.

Copywork

> And answering, the king will say to them, "Truly I say to you, as you did it to one of the least of my brethren, you did it to me."
>
> —Matthew 25:40

Parent's Help Page
A Saint and His Lion

Observation

1. Together with your child, find Ethiopia on the map. with your child.
2. Discuss the living conditions in Third World countries with your child.
3. Locate an issue of *National Geographic* to show your child how people in Third World countries live.

Discussion Answers

1. A "tukul" is a "hut of sticks and mud."
2. The king called Tekla's parents to his palace because there was a star shining over their "tukul."
3. Tekla was the name of one of the first Christians in Ethiopia.
4. Allow your child to tell you about the two incidents: when Tekla was almost injured at his christening and when he was injured when he fell out of the tree.
5. The Ethiopian word for "lion" is *Anbassa*.
6. Tekla left the monastery because he wanted to "be a shepherd of men" and "tell everyone about Jesus" to share the "good news of our holy faith."
7. Tekla couldn't make another crutch because he was in the desert where there was hardly any vegetation.
8. The lion did not attack him because he recognized Tekla as being the one who had helped him.
9. Yes, Tekla's parents were very proud of their son. Let the child explain why.

Enrichment Activities

1. Have your child describe the differences and similarities between our modern day cross and the Ethiopian Orthodox Church's cross as depicted in the book.

2. **Spiritual Sponsorship**: Now would be a good time to expose your child to the beautiful reality that we are all brothers and sisters in Christ and that the Catholic Church has members all over the world. Holding a globe, explain to your child that when he/she is at Mass in the United States, a little boy or girl in another country is also attending Mass. At the moment the host is consecrated, all the angels and saints in Heaven (yes, even St. Tekla of Ethiopia) as well as our family and that little boy or girl are joined together through the Holy Sacrifice of the Mass. What an amazing way to be connected—and what a great opportunity to pray for one another.

   Talk to your child about the many homeless and orphaned children in other countries—made so by natural disasters and war. If your family is financially able to, sponsoring a child is a beautiful way to open your hearts to a child who needs a share of the wealth that we enjoy in America.

   After talking to people and checking what is offered, I have been assured that Christian Foundation for Children and Aging at http://www.cfcausa.org/ is a worthy and reliable Catholic organization to sponsor through. For just a dollar a day, your sponsorship will assist this child with his education, food, clothing, and medical care. Letters and photographs may be exchanged with your sponsored children throughout the year. Many of these countries have a very rich Catholic culture and, I am told, the children write of wonderful Catholic feast day celebrations and observances. These exchanges can give your child a broader worldview and a deeper Christian connection to someone who needs his help outside his country. It also reinforces an appreciation for the freedom of religion which we are so blessed to have and, hopefully, teach your child how to celebrate the liturgical year with real appreciation. It is a spiritual adoption in the broadest sense. (The selection of this organization is the author's personal opinion. You will want to research the options available and select something that you feel is worthy and reputable.)

   Your child can select his very own brother or sister abroad. He can study his adopted brother/sister's country, culture, and lifestyle. He can offer up his candy or bag of chips in order to add money to the monthly fund.

Make a "blessing box" with your child using a shoebox. Wrap it in tissue paper and decorate it with materials found at the local craft/hobby store. Throughout the year, have your child place various items in the box to send to his adopted brother/sister on a predetermined date—perhaps on the Feast day of St. Tekla of Ethiopia (October 27) or on the Feast of the Epiphany.

Items to place in box:

- holy cards
- rosary
- religious medal
- prayer booklets
- small statue of Mary or a saint
- Christian Foundation offers a brochure that specifies the needs of overseas children, as well as what can be sent to them. *

If your family is unable to financially sponsor a child, your son or daughter can still become a spiritual sponsor. Check out the website at http://www.compassion.com/. Allow your son or daughter to view the photos and select a child he/she would like to pray for daily. Any financial sacrifices he makes during the year can be deposited in the blessing box. Then, at year's end, the blessing box funds can be sent to a charitable organization that takes care of needy children.

Whether you are able to help financially or spiritually—or both—take the time to make this universal Christian duty a part of your child's religious training. Discuss with your child how participating in this spiritual sponsorship is the same ministry St. Tekla of Ethiopia practiced. We imitate his example when we share the good news of the Gospels and care for the poor.

*Christian Foundation can also be contacted by calling (800) 875-6564 or by writing: Christian Foundation for Children and Aging, One Elmwood Ave., Kansas City, KS 66103,

Father Phillip Tells a Ghost Story
A Story of Divine Mercy
Written and Illustrated by Miriam Andrews Lademan/ Susan Andrews
Brindle
Published by Precious Life Books, Inc, 2004.
Cover reprinted by permission of the publisher.

FEAST DAY: ALL HALLOWS EVE, OCTOBER 31

Vocabulary

unison	salvation	offensive	solemn
atone	eternity	authentic	beatification
expiate	perplexed	venerate	pronounced

Discussion Questions

1. What special time of year are the O'Keefe children preparing for?
2. Where do certain souls go after death?
3. Why are they called the *Poor* Souls?
4. What is the most frightening thing in the world?
5. Which ghost stories should we stay away from?
6. Why do the Holy Souls in Purgatory come to Earth?
7. What can the Holy Souls in Heaven do for us?
8. How can we help the Poor Souls in Purgatory?
9. In the picture of the Divine Mercy, what does the pale ray represent and what does the red ray represent?
10. What does the word "Halloween" really mean?
11. What happens on All Soul's Day?

Copywork

Dear Jesus, I'm suffering for You, please help the
Poor Souls in Purgatory.
—Words Father Phillip teaches the children
in *FatherPhillip Tells a Ghost Story*

Parent's Help Page
Father Phillip Tells a Ghost Story

Observation

1. This story can be a springboard to other stories you might pursue with your children.
   a) Sister Faustina and the story of the Divine Mercy of Christ (See *Helen's Special Picture* by David Previtali
   b) The Polish Prince, his former steward and the steward's wife
   c) Pope Gregory and the gentle, kind servant
   d) St. Gertrude and the devil's temptation
   e) Servant girl in France and the kind young man
2. Look at the first picture. What season is it? (Autumn) What are the children doing? (carving pumpkins, playing ball, riding in the wagon) Notice the girl in the far back by the grotto. Why do you think she is there? (She is leaving a bouquet of flowers at the statue of the Blessed Mother.)

Discussion Answers

1. They are preparing for Halloween and the Feast of All Saints.

2. Certain souls go to purgatory after death.
3. They are called the Poor Souls because they suffer very much in Purgatory and are often forgotten by the living on Earth. Without our prayers and sacrifice, they have to suffer longer in Purgatory.
4. The most frightening thing in the world is the people on Earth who are indifferent to God.
5. We should stay away from ghost stories that are associated with evil acts.
6. The Holy Souls in Purgatory come to Earth to assist the living and make atonement for their sins.
7. The Holy Souls in Heaven can pray for us and intercede on our behalf.
8. We can help the Poor Souls in Purgatory by praying, having Masses said for them, and offering up our hurts and sufferings for them.
9. In the Divine Mercy picture, the pale ray represents Water and the red ray represents Blood.
10. "Halloween" really means "eve of the holy day" because it is the night before All Saints' Day.
11. On All Souls Days, a great number of souls enter into the glory of Heaven.

Enrichment Activity

Here is an activity you can do to help your child visualize the idea of the Communion of Saints. Explain that we are part of the mystical body of Christ which includes three parts:

1. The Souls on Earth are the Church Militant—we are still in the spiritual fight for Christ.
2. The Poor Souls in Purgatory are the Church Suffering—they are suffering for the sins committed on Earth.
3. The Holy Souls in Heaven are the Church Triumphant—they are the souls that have triumphantly made it to Heaven.

Using masking tape, make a large triangle on your floor or table top. Put a picture or drawing of God at the very top. Check around the house for saint prayer cards and angel pictures or figurines (look in your Christmas Nativity set). Place them at the top of the triangle. (Church Triumphant)

Locate pictures of family members or friends who have died. Prayer cards from the funeral are good to use. Also, find any crosses or crucifixes that you have. Place these in the middle of the triangle. (Church Suffering)

Locate pictures of your child and family and some plastic army soldiers. Place these pictures at the bottom of the triangle and place an army soldier on top of each picture. (Church Militant)

November

Sean Fitzpatrick

184

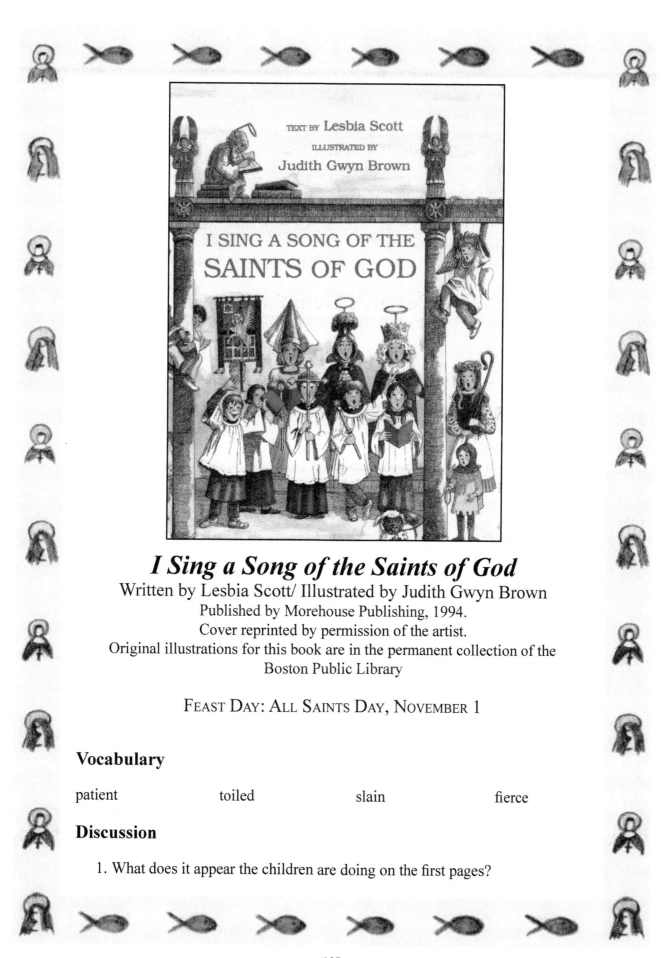

I Sing a Song of the Saints of God

Written by Lesbia Scott/ Illustrated by Judith Gwyn Brown
Published by Morehouse Publishing, 1994.
Cover reprinted by permission of the artist.
Original illustrations for this book are in the permanent collection of the
Boston Public Library

FEAST DAY: ALL SAINTS DAY, NOVEMBER 1

Vocabulary

patient   toiled   slain   fierce

Discussion

1. What does it appear the children are doing on the first pages?

2. Who are today's saints?
3. Who is your favorite saint?
4. What do you like to do or what do you want to be when you grow up? Look up the patron saint for that skill or job.

Copywork

All ye holy men and women, Saints of God, make intercession for us.

—from the "Litany of the Saints," traditional.

Parent's Help Page
I Sing a Song of the Saints of God

Observation

Take a moment to observe the saints in the book and discuss what they are doing.

St. Luke—Doctor
St. Margaret—Queen
St. Joan of Arc—Shepherdess
St. Martin of Tours—Soldier
St. Ignatius of Antioch—Slain by a Wild Beast

Please note that the author lists John Donne, however, he is not a Catholic saint.
Please keep this in mind as you are sharing this book with your child.

Discussion Answers

1. The children are planning to put on a play.
2. Today's saints are those who love to do Jesus' will. They can be teachers, sailors, our neighbors . . . even *you.*
3. Expose your child to many different saints so he can decide which is his favorite.
4. Listen to your child and help him focus on the things he does well.

Enrichment Activities

1. Research your favorite saint or patron saint and give a narrative about him/her.
2. Go to Illuminated Ink's website and review Saint Symbols. Can you find the symbol for your saint? http://www.illuminatedink.com/saint_symbols/

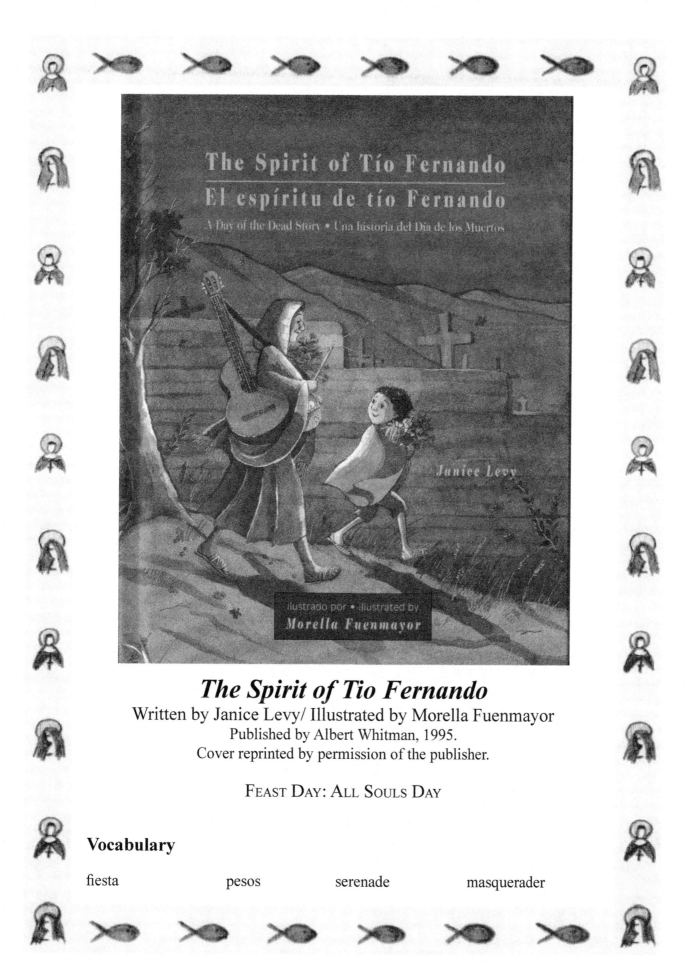

The Spirit of Tio Fernando

Written by Janice Levy/ Illustrated by Morella Fuenmayor
Published by Albert Whitman, 1995.
Cover reprinted by permission of the publisher.

Feast Day: All Souls Day

Vocabulary

fiesta   pesos   serenade   masquerader

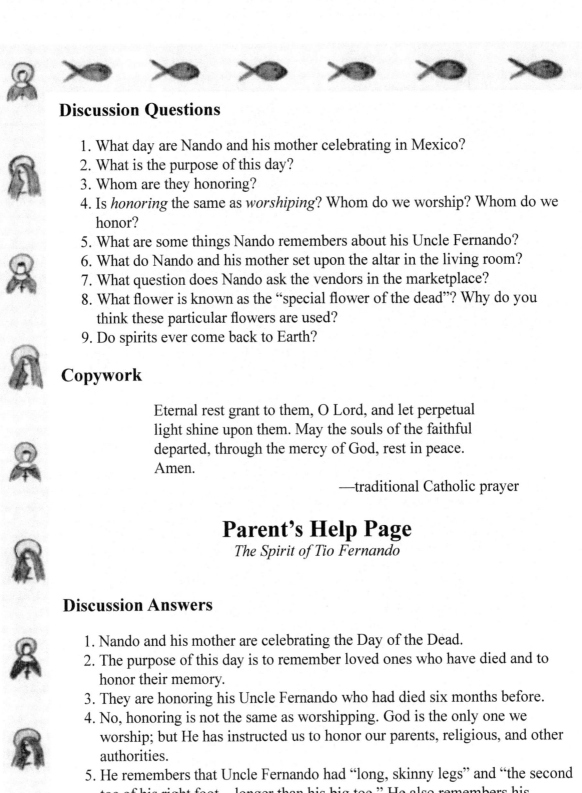

Discussion Questions

1. What day are Nando and his mother celebrating in Mexico?
2. What is the purpose of this day?
3. Whom are they honoring?
4. Is *honoring* the same as *worshiping*? Whom do we worship? Whom do we honor?
5. What are some things Nando remembers about his Uncle Fernando?
6. What do Nando and his mother set upon the altar in the living room?
7. What question does Nando ask the vendors in the marketplace?
8. What flower is known as the "special flower of the dead"? Why do you think these particular flowers are used?
9. Do spirits ever come back to Earth?

Copywork

Eternal rest grant to them, O Lord, and let perpetual light shine upon them. May the souls of the faithful departed, through the mercy of God, rest in peace. Amen.

—traditional Catholic prayer

Parent's Help Page
The Spirit of Tio Fernando

Discussion Answers

1. Nando and his mother are celebrating the Day of the Dead.
2. The purpose of this day is to remember loved ones who have died and to honor their memory.
3. They are honoring his Uncle Fernando who had died six months before.
4. No, honoring is not the same as worshipping. God is the only one we worship; but He has instructed us to honor our parents, religious, and other authorities.
5. He remembers that Uncle Fernando had "long, skinny legs" and "the second toe of his right foot…longer than his big toe." He also remembers his having a moustache and bringing Nando coconut candy.
6. Upon the altar, Nando and his mother set pictures of Uncle Fernando, his favorite foods, and his wooden flute.
7. Nando asks everyone in the marketplace, "How will I meet Tio Fernando's spirit?"

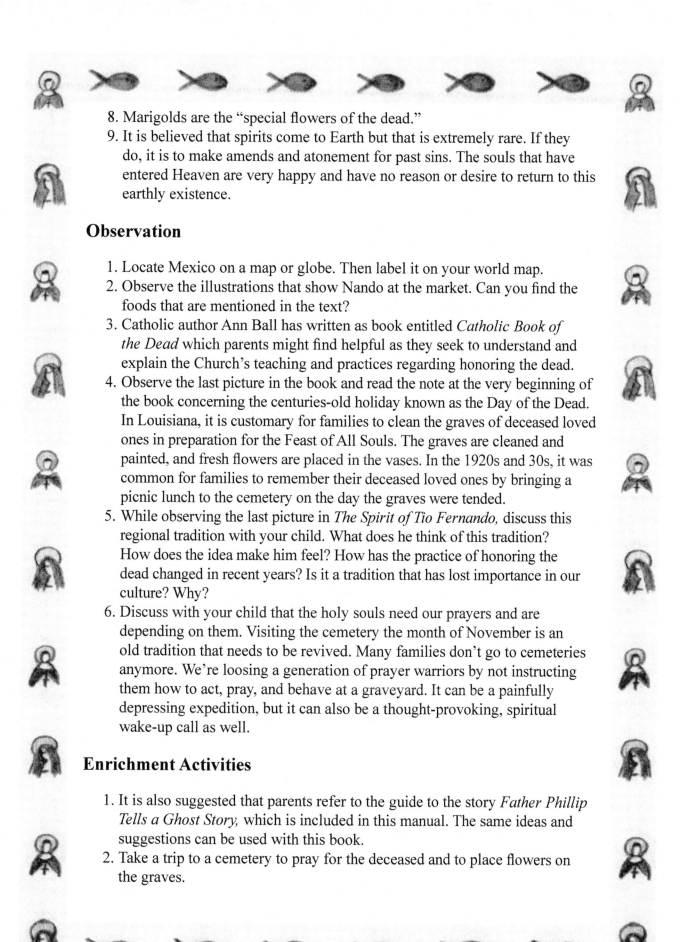

8. Marigolds are the "special flowers of the dead."
9. It is believed that spirits come to Earth but that is extremely rare. If they do, it is to make amends and atonement for past sins. The souls that have entered Heaven are very happy and have no reason or desire to return to this earthly existence.

Observation

1. Locate Mexico on a map or globe. Then label it on your world map.
2. Observe the illustrations that show Nando at the market. Can you find the foods that are mentioned in the text?
3. Catholic author Ann Ball has written as book entitled *Catholic Book of the Dead* which parents might find helpful as they seek to understand and explain the Church's teaching and practices regarding honoring the dead.
4. Observe the last picture in the book and read the note at the very beginning of the book concerning the centuries-old holiday known as the Day of the Dead. In Louisiana, it is customary for families to clean the graves of deceased loved ones in preparation for the Feast of All Souls. The graves are cleaned and painted, and fresh flowers are placed in the vases. In the 1920s and 30s, it was common for families to remember their deceased loved ones by bringing a picnic lunch to the cemetery on the day the graves were tended.
5. While observing the last picture in *The Spirit of Tio Fernando,* discuss this regional tradition with your child. What does he think of this tradition? How does the idea make him feel? How has the practice of honoring the dead changed in recent years? Is it a tradition that has lost importance in our culture? Why?
6. Discuss with your child that the holy souls need our prayers and are depending on them. Visiting the cemetery the month of November is an old tradition that needs to be revived. Many families don't go to cemeteries anymore. We're loosing a generation of prayer warriors by not instructing them how to act, pray, and behave at a graveyard. It can be a painfully depressing expedition, but it can also be a thought-provoking, spiritual wake-up call as well.

Enrichment Activities

1. It is also suggested that parents refer to the guide to the story *Father Phillip Tells a Ghost Story,* which is included in this manual. The same ideas and suggestions can be used with this book.
2. Take a trip to a cemetery to pray for the deceased and to place flowers on the graves.

Catholic children need to know that certain behavior is expected at the cemetery. They should be taught proper etiquette before visiting a cemetery. Reminders should be given before they step out of the vehicle:

- Be respectful and reverent.
- This is not a park or playground; it is a resting place.
- Walk slowly between graves (not on them), and pray the rosary (no running or jumping allowed).
- Leave devotional items on the graves and straighten flowers and vases; do not remove anything.
- Do not litter.
- Show the same reverence you would in a church and the same respect you would have in a hospital.

Catholics can obtain a partial indulgence when visiting the cemetery in respectful silence and devout prayer. Plenary indulgences can be obtained for the poor souls in purgatory by visiting a cemetery between November 1-November 8.

Doing a variety of small gestures when passing or visiting a cemetery should also be encouraged:
- making the sign of the cross,
- saying a rosary,
- praying the Eternal Rest (Requiem Aeternam) prayer (see the copywork selection).

3. While visiting a cemetery, you may try to do stone rubbings. Place a sheet of paper over an image on the grave stone, place a crayon sideways on the stone and rub it across the image. The image will show up on the paper.

4. Fold a piece of gray construction paper in half. Cut an arched tombstone from it. Draw a cross on the front and outline it in silver glitter. Inside the paper stone, write the names of family members who have died or paste funeral cards inside of it. Place this inside your Liturgical Year Notebook.

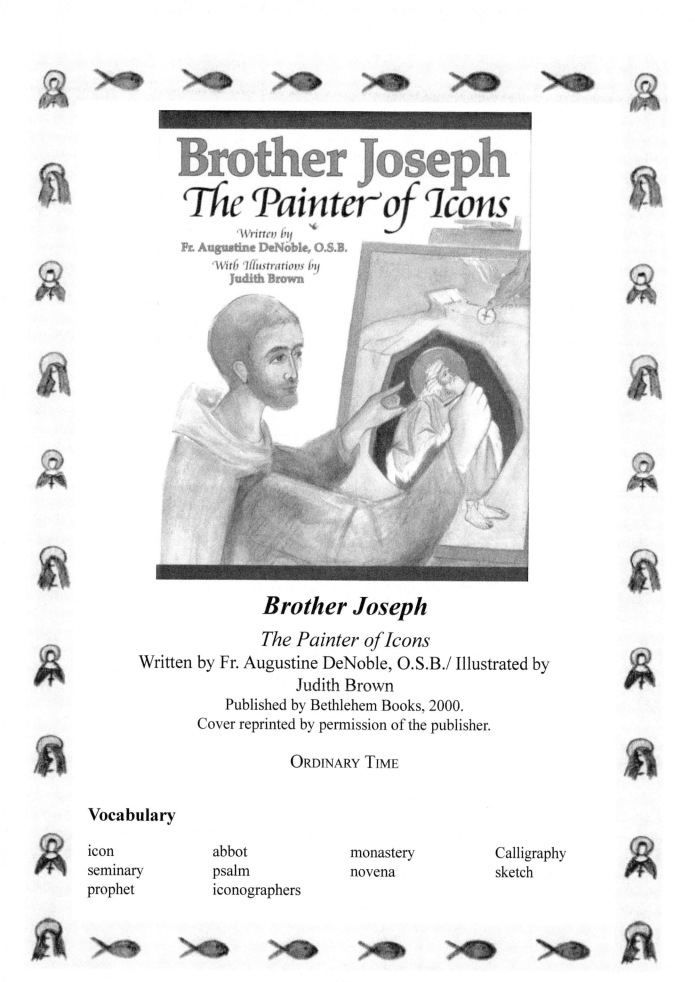

Brother Joseph

The Painter of Icons
Written by Fr. Augustine DeNoble, O.S.B./ Illustrated by
Judith Brown
Published by Bethlehem Books, 2000.
Cover reprinted by permission of the publisher.

ORDINARY TIME

Vocabulary

icon	abbot	monastery	Calligraphy
seminary	psalm	novena	sketch
prophet	iconographers		

Discussion Questions

1. Whose artistic work inspired Tom?
2. Who is the Good Shepherd? (Read John 10:11,14.)
3. What is meant by the "Paschal Lamb"?
4. Who takes Jesus' place here on Earth and watches over His flock?
5. Who was the first pope?
6. Who is our pope today?
7. Who was Elijah? (Read 1 Kings 17-19.)

Copywork

My brush will up and downward go,
I'll paint like Fra Angelico!
—the words of Brother Joseph in *Brother Joseph,*
The Painter of Icons

Parent's Help Page
Brother Joseph, Painter of Icons

Discussion Answers

1. Fra Angelico's work inspired Tom.
2. The good shepherd is Jesus.
3. The Pascal Lamb is a symbol between the lamb sacrificed and consumed at the Passover Feast and the "Lamb of God" (our Savior and Redeemer) who shed His blood for the salvation of the world.
4. The Pope takes Jesus place on earth under the influence of the Holy Spirit.
5. St. Peter was the first pope.
6. At the time of this writing, St. Benedict the XVI is our pope. (Make sure your child knows the pope's name)
7. Elijah was a great prophet.

Enrichment Activities

1. Locate Italy on a world map or globe. Then label it on your world or Europe map.
2. Read the parable of the Good Shepherd. Have a statue or picture of this on hand and discuss with your child the picture on page 13 in *Brother Joseph, Painter of Icons*.

3. Find examples of calligraphy in Brother Joseph, Painter of Icons (see pages 8, 11, 14, 16, 21).

4. Read about Elijah and the "chariot of fire" in 2 Kings 2:11 while your child looks at the picture on pages 22-23 in *Brother Joseph, Painter of Icons.*

5. Write a composition about the things that you are "busy with" that bring much joy and peace to others.

6. Try this art lesson. Place a key, a coin, a leaf, a scapular medal, or a rosary crucifix under drawing paper. Rub a crayon over them to make an impression.

7. Check this site for information about painting with egg-tempera: http://www.eggtempera.com/intro.html

8. Plan a family picnic and go cloud watching. Trace pictures in the clouds.

9. Read "A Note from the Publisher" on the copyright page of *Brother Joseph, Painter of Icons.* Define "painter" and "writer" and then compare/contrast the two.

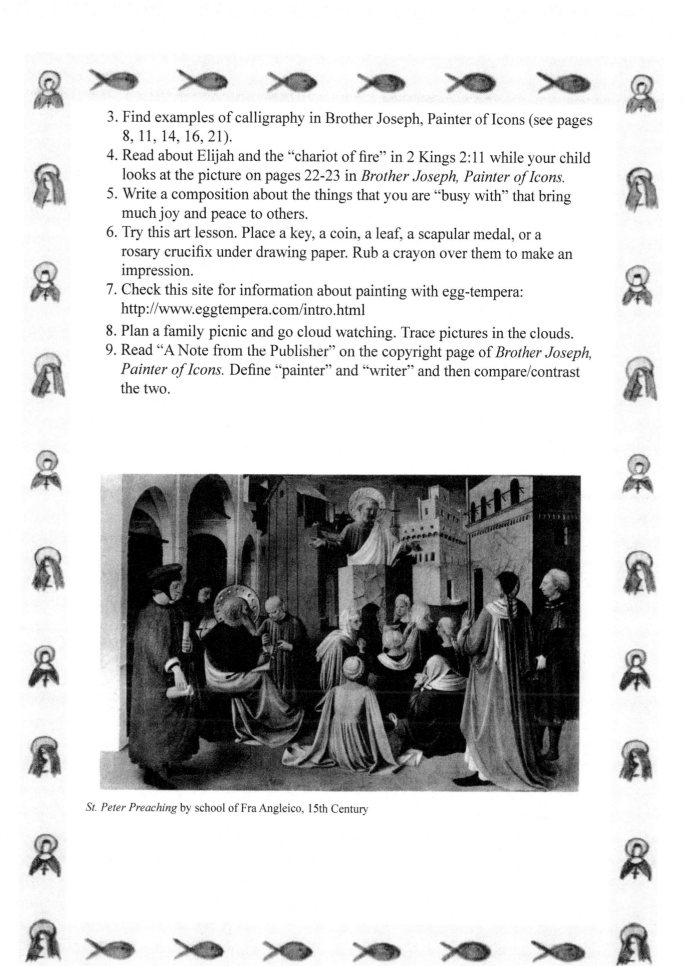

St. Peter Preaching by school of Fra Angleico, 15th Century

194

December

Sean Fitzpatrick

Maureen Van Nostrand

Saint Francis and the Christmas Donkey
Written and Illustrated by Robert Byrd

ADVENT

Vocabulary

vow	patient	scraggly	summon
curiosity	scrawny	scoff	tidings

Discussion Questions

1. Why did St. Francis talk to the animals?
2. What was the donkey complaining about?
3. Describe the donkey in the beginning of creation.
4. Why did the other animals get upset with Donkey?
5. What was his sin?
6. What special job did donkey have in Bethlehem?

7. What gift did the donkey give the baby Jesus?
8. What made the donkey feel accepted and loved after his sacrifice to the baby Jesus?

Parent's Help Page
Saint Francis and the Christmas Donkey

Observation

Allow your child time to simply look at the animal pictures if he/she wants to. Notice all the different ways that donkeys have been used in different cultures and times.

Discussion Answers

1. St. Francis believed all God's creatures were precious to God and should be treated with kindness *"from the tiniest mouse to the powerful great gray wolf."* He believed that we should *"respect and honor all living things"* because they are gifts from God to us.
2. The donkey complained that his work was hard and others make fun of the way he sounds.
3. The donkey was handsome with delicate ears and a tiny tail, and had a beautiful voice.
4. He was always laughing and making fun of them.
5. The sin of pride. Discuss with your child how the sin of pride was Satan's downfall and we must guard against becoming prideful creatures ourselves. Satan was unable to bow down to a mere man (Jesus) and refused to do so. Thus he was banished from Heaven. Jesus came to earth as a servant to men. We are called to follow his example and serve others instead of ourselves.
6. The donkey brought Joseph and Mary to Bethlehem.
7. The donkey gave Jesus the gifts of love, devotion, and courage.
8. The donkey *"felt the gentleness of the other animals. And in his own heart, in his very own way, the donkey knew what he had done, and he was happy."*

Enrichment Activity

1. If you have preschoolers, have them wiggle like a worm or fish, hop like a frog, crawl like a turtle, do the crab walk, bark like a dog, meow like a cat, moo like a cow, roar like a bear.

2. Create an Advent calendar using a picture of Mary on the donkey with Joseph at her side. Photocopy or trace the graphic printed below. Have the child color it. You may want to laminate it or glue it onto stiff cardboard so it will last for all of Advent. Draw a calendar on a large piece of paper and move the threesome forward for each day before Christmas. Place stickers, magazine pictures, drawings of the other animals on each calendar day as the threesome pass them. (So as the threesome moves to December 4, let's say, place an animal on December 3.) You will to think of a lot of animals to fill in the spaces. As the calendar is filled, it symbolizes all creation waiting for Our Lord's coming.

Permission to photocopy granted, Catholic Mosaic, Hillside Education ©2006

The Clown of God

Written and Illustrated by Tomie dePaola

© 1978 by Tomie dePaola, reprintd by permission Harcourt Inc.

ADVENT

Vocabulary

ragamuffin   maestro   sacrilege   monastery

Discussion Questions

1. What did Giovanni call his golden ball?
2. Can you think of another saint who liked to envision herself as a little ball that the Christ Child could play with?
3. What do words of the Little Brothers of St. Francis mean when they say, *If you give happiness to people, you give glory to God as well*?
4. What small act can *you* do to give glory to God?
5. Look at the back of the book to see what art medium artist Tomie dePaola used to make the drawings in *Clown of God*.
6. Ask your mom for fruits and vegetables to juggle. Is it as easy as you thought it'd be? Or harder?

Copywork

If you give happiness to people, you give glory to God as well.

—from *Clown of God* by Tomie dePaola

Parent's Help Page
The Clown of God

Discussion Answers

1. The golden ball was called *"The Sun in the Heavens!"*
2. St. Therese, the Little Flower, likened herself to a ball that Christ played with.
3. Let the child explain what he thinks about the quote. Probe for deeper answers if needed. Giovanni's juggling gives glory to God because he uses the gifts that God give him to make people happy.
4. Discuss with your child the small acts he or she can do each day to give glory to God. (Make bed, pick up toys, or play or help younger siblings, and so on.)
5. It reads: *"The drawings were done in pencil, ink, and watercolor on Fabriano 140-lb. handmade watercolor paper."*
6. Let your child tell you what he or she thinks about juggling.

Enrichment Activity

1. Draw a picture of yourself doing something that you do well. At the bottom write how this is your gift to the baby Jesus. Place it in your Liturgical Notebook.
2. During Advent, make a little offering of something for Baby Jesus everyday.

The Miracle of Saint Nicholas
Written by Gloria Whelan/ Illustrated by Judith Brown

ADVENT

Vocabulary

babushka   icon   miracle   tramp   kutya

Discussion Questions

1. How old was Babushka's icon of St. Nicholas?
2. What happened after the soldiers barred the doors of St. Nicholas Church?

3. How long had the church been closed?
4. What did the shoemaker say about Alexi because of his worn boots? What do you think he means?
5. When did Alexi's mother say the kutya was done? What did she mean by this?
6. Why did Alexi's father spread straw on the floor and hay under the tablecloth?
7. What did Alexi and Natasha receive on Christmas Eve? Compare these to the things children of today receive on Christmas.
8. What was the shoemaker's big secret?
9. What did he carry into the church?
10. Did Alexi's babushka's dream come true?

Copywork

> A miracle happens when God enters into your
> dream. But first you must have the dream.
>
> —the words of Babushka to Alexi in *The Miracle of St. Nicholas*

Parent's Help Page
The Miracle of Saint Nicholas)

Observation

1. Since this book is illustrated by the same artist as *Brother Joseph: Painter of Icons,* you may want to revisit that story.
2. Study the picture of Alexi sweeping in the church. What do you see behind him?
3. Look at the picture of the St. Nicholas icon in this book. Describe it.
4. When the villagers left Alexi cleaning in the church, they left with smiles and secrets. Go back through the book and have your child remember what secrets each person brought:

Farmer and family—two silver candlesticks
Farmer's wife—handful of candles
Teacher—a beautiful altar cloth
Carpenter and his family—a cross
Storekeeper and his wife—a bottle of wine and a basket of holy Christmas bread
Alexi's babushka—the icon of St. Nicholas

5. Observe the pictures of the shoemaker as a priest. Discuss with your child how there was a time in Russia's history when being a priest was dangerous. Discuss how priests were often captured, tortured, arrested, beaten, and even killed. Perhaps look into the history of the Cure of Ars and see how, as a young boy, he lived during a time when it was dangerous to be a priest in France. Discuss how priests might be viewed as threats to a country's ruling political party?

Discussion Answers

1. The icon was 500 years old.
2. When the doors of St. Nicholas were barred, everything inside the church disappeared.
3. The church had been closed for 60 years.
4. The shoemaker said, "There is a boy who will always be one step ahead of us." Let the child say what he/she thinks of this statement.
5. The kutya was done when it "does not talk anymore." She meant when it quit bubbling.
6. Alexi's father spread straw on the floor "to remind them that Jesus was born in a stable" and under the table cloth "to remind them Jesus lay in a manger."
7. Alexi received new boots. Natasha received a sweater. They both received a gingerbread man. Answers will vary on what children today receive.
8. The shoemaker was really a priest!
9. He carried the Holy Scriptures.
10. Yes, babushka's dream came true.

Enrichment Activity

1. Find Russia on a map or globe. Then label it on your map.
2. Count how many times an icon appears in this storybook.
3. Attempt to draw an icon and add your drawing to your Liturgical Year Notebook. You may want to find some books on icons at the library to have on hand during this book study.

The Lady of Guadalupe
Written and Illustrated by Tomie dePaola

Feast Day: December 12th

Vocabulary

Friars	crescent	interpreter
trudged	tilma	abode

Discussion Questions

1. Who was Juan Diego?
2. Why was his name changed from "He-who-speaks-like-an-eagle"?
3. Why did Juan Diego climb the hill of Tepeyac?
4. Whom did the Mother of God send Juan to see and what was her request?
5. What is an interpreter?
6. Why did Juan Diego think that Mary should send someone else to the Bishop?
7. Why do you think Mary chose Juan Diego?
8. Why did the Bishop ask for a sign? What sign did he ask for?
9. What do you think the servants meant when they said, "This Juan Diego is a wizard-half-tiger with the wings of an eagle"?
10. What did Juan Diego find upon returning home?
11. What are some of the folk remedies the villagers used in their attempts to cure Juan's uncle?
12. Why did Juan avoid the hill of Tepeyac? Do you think you would have done the same thing?
13. What was so miraculous about roses growing on the hill of Tepeyac?
14. Describe the image that was miraculously imprinted on Juan Diego's tilma.
15. When is Juan Diego's feast day celebrated?
16. What day is the feast day of Our Lady of Guadalupe?
17. What does *Guadalupe* mean?

Copywork

May God be as good to you as he was to Juan Diego.

—what Mexican families tell newborn children,
from *Our Lady of Guadalupe* by Tomie dePaola

Parent's Help Page
The Lady of Guadalupe

Discussion Answers

1. Juan Diego was a simple, Indian farmer living in Mexico.
2. His name was changed to Juan Diego when he became a Christian.
3. Juan saw a "brilliant white cloud" and climbed the hill to have a closer look.
4. The Mother of God sent Juan to see the Bishop of Mexico. Her request was that a church be built on the hill of Tepeyac.

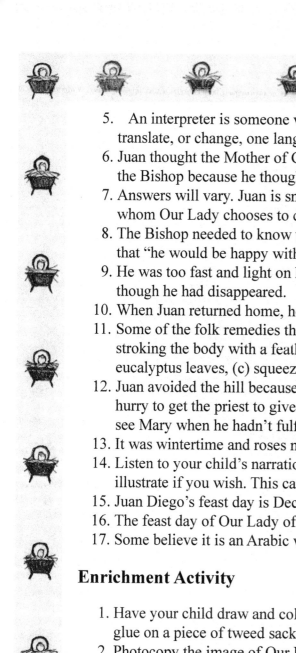

5. An interpreter is someone who knows more than one language and can translate, or change, one language into another

6. Juan thought the Mother of God should send a child or a noble person to see the Bishop because he thought he was not worthy.

7. Answers will vary. Juan is small and poor and it is those souls through whom Our Lady chooses to do great things.

8. The Bishop needed to know that this apparition was truly Our Lady. He said that "he would be happy with any sort of sign the Lady chose to send him."

9. He was too fast and light on his feet for them to keep up with. It was as though he had disappeared.

10. When Juan returned home, he found his uncle very ill.

11. Some of the folk remedies the Indians used to cure the uncle were (a) stroking the body with a feather and egg, (b) administering herb tea and eucalyptus leaves, (c) squeezing the fever out of the body using scarves.

12. Juan avoided the hill because he feared his uncle was dying and was in a hurry to get the priest to give his uncle the Last Blessings. He didn't want to see Mary when he hadn't fulfilled her request.

13. It was wintertime and roses never grew on the hillside.

14. Listen to your child's narration of the image. Write it down for him to illustrate if you wish. This can be placed in his Liturgical Year Notebook.

15. Juan Diego's feast day is December 9.

16. The feast day of Our Lady of Guadalupe is December 12.

17. Some believe it is an Arabic word that means "hidden river."

Enrichment Activity

1. Have your child draw and color a Lady of Guadalupe image, cut out and glue on a piece of tweed sackcloth.

2. Photocopy the image of Our Lady of Guadalupe on the previous page, or find an image in a coloring book, and have the child color it and cut it out. Glue it onto red or green construction paper and outline it with gold pen or glitter. Place it in the Liturgical Year Notebook.

3. Illuminated Ink (http://www.illuminatedink.com/products/4/12/) sells a lovely craft for making a Marian shrine of Our Lady Guadalupe.

The Legend of the Poinsettia
Written and Illustrated by Tomie dePaola

ADVENT

Vocabulary

burro	tortilla	shrine	fiesta
loom	weave	aisle	procession

Discussion Questions

1. What was the name of Lucida's house?
2. Why did Lucida, Paco, and Lupe go each evening to the shrine of the Virgin of Guadalupe?
3. What is another name for "Christmas"?
4. What did Padre Alvarez ask of Lucida's mother?
5. Why was Lucida's mother unable to finish the blanket in time for the Christmas procession?
6. What did Lucida find to offer the Christ Child?
7. What happened to the plain weeds Lucida had laid around the stable?
8. Poinsettias are also know as *la Flor de Nochebuena*. What does this phrase mean?

Copywork

Any gift is beautiful because it is given.
—from *The Legend of the Poinsettia* by Tomie dePaola

Parent's Help Page
(The Legend of the Poinsettia)

Observation

If you have already read *The Lady of Guadalupe* by Tomie dePaola, see if your child remembers the story and recognizes the statue near the front gate in this story.

At Christmas time, look closely at a real poinsettia. The red parts are not really flowers. They are the leaves that have turned red. Did you know that it was believed for years that poinsettia plants were poisonous? This proved to be a myth. Still, it is said that poinsettias are very bitter and were never meant to be eaten. Use poinsettias for decoration around the house—enjoy their beauty.

Discussion Answers

1. Lucida's house was called a *casita*.
2. They went to the shrine to see if fresh candles were needed.
3. Another name for "Christmas" is *la Navidad*.
4. Padre Alvarez asked Lucida's mother to make a new blanket to cover the Baby Jesus.

5. She could not finish the blanket because she became sick.
6. Lucida found a patch of tall green weeds.
7. The weeds became flaming red stars.
8. *La Flor de Nochebuena* means "Flower of the Holy Night."

Enrichment Activities

1. Make paper poinsettias following the directions below. All you need is red paper. Construction paper works, but a lighter weight paper is better. When you are done write on the back what gift *you* could bring the Baby Jesus. Place it in your Liturgical Year Notebook. You may make several of them to decorate the manger scene in your house.

   a. Square the paper by folding it in half diagonally and then cutting off the excess.

   b. Open it and fold it in half lengthwise and then again so you have a small square.

   c. Here is the key to be sure the poinsettia turns out correctly. Once you have a small square, one corner will be all "folds." The other three corners will have open edges. Turn the paper so that the "folds" corner is at the bottom. Now it looks like a diamond.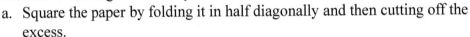

   d. Fold the right corner side of the diamond to the left, keeping the "folds" corner at the bottom. You should now have a long triangle.

   e. Cut the triangle through all thicknesses along the lines shown below.

   f. Your paper still looks like a diamond. On the right and left sides, cut two half circles. This creates the petals. You can adjust the size of the petals by making the half circles larger or smaller. Punch a hole in the diamond as shown near the folds corner. This hole is optional. Open up the paper and see the poinsettia you have made.

The Donkey's Dream
Written and Illustrated by Barbara Helen Berger

CHRISTMAS DAY

Discussion Questions

1. What did the donkey hear in the city?
2. What baby do you think was crying?
3. What did the shop rock like?
4. What baby would the ship have rocked to sleep?
5. What child do you think the donkey heard laughing?
6. Who stood around the rose?
7. What came out to greet the couple when they reached town?
8. Why was the donkey suddenly not tired when he saw the baby?

Copywork

Mystical Rose, pray for us.
Tower of David, pray for us.

—from the Litany of Mary, Traditional

Parent's Help Page
The Donkey's Dream

Observation

1. See if your child can recite, in order, the visions the donkey saw in his dream:
   a) a city with gates, towers, and domes
   b) a ship
   c) a fountain
   d) a rose
   e) a lady full of heaven
2. Read the *Author's Note* in the back of book and discuss it with your child.

Discussion Answers

1. The donkey heard a child crying.
2. It was Baby Jesus
3. The ship rocked like a cradle.
4. It would have rocked Baby Jesus
5. It was the Christ Child
6. Angels stood around the rose.
7. Only dogs came out to greet them.
8. Once again we are reminded that Jesus' "yoke is easy" and "his burden is light" (see copywork for *The Last Straw*). The donkey was no longer tired because he had carried The Christ Child upon his back and Christ takes away all our burdens and concerns.

Enrichment Activity

Together with your child recite the Litany of Mary, from which the names of Mary used in this book were taken (see Appendix A). See if he can visualize some of the names of Mary as the donkey did. Illustrate a few and place them in the Liturgical Year Notebook.

The Crippled Lamb
Written by Max Lucado/ Illustrated by Liz Bonahm

CHRISTMAS DAY

Vocabulary

blotch   hobble   limp   timid

Discussion Questions

1. Why was the little lamb sad?
2. Who was Josh's best friend? What kind of animal was she?
3. What did Josh and Abigail do together?
4. What did Abigail tell Josh several times?
5. Why did the shepherds move the sheep?
6. Have you ever heard the saying, "The grass is always greener on the other side"? What does this mean to you? Do you think that's the way Josh felt while watching the other sheep in the green meadow, since he himself had to stay behind at the stable?
7. What woke Josh up? Whom did he see in the stable with him and Abigail?
8. Why was the baby crying? How did Josh help him?
9. What made Josh feel special?
10. Where is our special place?

Copywork

> The Lord is my Shepherd; I shall not want
> He maketh me to lie down in green pastures:
> He leadeth me beside the still waters.
> He restoreth my soul:
> He leadeth me in the paths of righteousness
>   for His name's sake.
>
> —Psalm 23:1-3

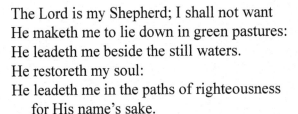

Parent's Help Page
(The Crippled Lamb)

Observation

Observe the picture on the page where a shepherd is talking to Josh with his hand under Josh's chin. Whom does the shepherd remind you of? What is another name that Jesus is known by? (*The Good Shepherd*) Do you have a statue of the Good Shepherd in your home? Jesus is a shepherd to His people. Like a good shepherd watches over his flock, Jesus watches over all of us.

Jesus is also known as the Paschal Lamb, a lamb who is offered up as a sacrifice to redeem the people. How was Jesus offered as a sacrifice to redeem us? Jesus was sacrificed on the cross because of our sins. He sacrificed Himself so that we might all find eternal happiness in Heaven with Him.

Discussion Answers

1. The little lamb was sad because 1) he was not snow-white like the other little lambs; 2) he didn't have a mom or dad; and 3) because he was cripple he could not run or jump.
2. Josh's best friend was Abigail. Abigail was an old cow.
3. Josh and Abigail would pretend they were on adventures and tell each other stories.
4. Abigail told Josh that God had a special place for those who feel left out.
5. The shepherd moved the sheep to a grassier area.
6. Discuss with your child the meaning behind the saying, "The grass is always greener on the other side," and how the grass isn't necessarily greener—it just seems that way.
7. Josh heard strange noises. He saw a baby in the feed box and a woman resting on a pile of hay.
8. The baby was crying because he was cold. Josh curled up beside him to warm him.
9. Josh was one of the first to welcome Jesus into the world.
10. Like Josh, we have a special place beside Jesus, our Lord.

Enrichment Activity

This is a good chance to look into Moira Farrell's Catholic albums that present the beautiful Montessori method catechism program, *Catechesis of the Good Shepherd.* These albums describe effective ways to help your child see Jesus as the Good Shepherd.

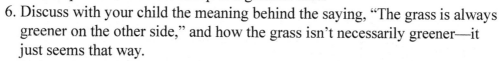

Appendices

Appendix A Prayers and Feast Days

1. Marian Feast Days and Apparitions

(Refer to this site for more dates and information:
http://www.catholic-forum.com/Saints/saintbvm.htm):

Mary, Mother of God—January 1
Espousal of the Virgin Mary—January 21
Nuestra Senora de la Altagracia—January 21
Purification of Mary—February 2
Our Lady of Lourdes—February 11
Annunciation—March 25
Our Lady of Częstochowa (the Black Madonna)—April 1
Month Dedicated to Mary—May
Our Lady of Fatima—May 13
Our Lady, Mediatrix of all Graces—May 31
Virgin Mother of Grace—June 9
Our Lady of Mount Carmel—July 16
Mary's Assumption into Heaven—August 15
Our Lady of Knock—August 21
Queenship of Mary—August 22
Blessed Mother's Birthday—September 8
Our Lady of Sorrows—September 15
Our Lady of LaSalette—September 19
Our Lady of the Rosary—October 7
Our Lady of the Miraculous Medal—November 27
Mary's Immaculate Conception—December 8
Our Lady of Guadalupe—December 12

2. Prayers

The Peace Prayer of Saint Francis

"O Lord, make me an instrument of Thy Peace!

> Where there is hatred, let me sow love.
> Where there is injury, pardon.
> Where there is discord, harmony.
> Where there is doubt, faith.
> Where there is despair, hope.
> Where there is darkness, light.
> Where there is sorrow, joy.

Oh Divine Master, grant that I may not
so much seek to be consoled as to console;
to be understood as to understand;
to be loved as to love;
for it is in giving that we receive;
it is in pardoning that we are pardoned;
and it is in dying that we are born to Eternal Life."

Another Prayer by St. Francis

Most high, glorious God,
enlighten the darkness of my heart
and give me Lord, a correct faith, a certain hope,
a perfect charity, sense and knowledge,
so that I may carry out Your holy and true command.
Amen

Anima Christi

Soul of Christ, sanctify me
Body of Christ, save me
Blood of Christ, inebriate me
Water from Christ's side, wash me
Passion of Christ, strengthen me
O good Jesus, hear me
Within Thy wounds hide me
Suffer me not to be separated from Thee
From the malicious enemy defend me
In the hour of my death call me
And bid me come unto Thee
"That I may praise Thee with Thy saints and with Thy angels"
"Forever and ever. Amen."

—attributed to St. Ignatius of Loyola"

Litany of Mary

Lord, have mercy on us. Christ have mercy on us.

Lord, have mercy on us.

Christ, hear us.

Christ graciously hear us.

God, the Father of heaven, have mercy on us.

God the Son, Redeemer of the world, have mercy on us.

God the Holy Ghost, have mercy on us.

Holy Trinity, one God, have mercy on us.

Holy Mary, pray for us.

Holy Mother of God, pray for us.

Holy Virgin of virgins, pray for us.

Mother of Christ, pray for us.

Mother of divine grace, pray for us.

Mother most pure, pray for us.

Mother most chaste, pray for us.

Mother inviolate, pray for us.

Mother undefiled, pray for us.

Mother most amiable, pray for us.

Mother most admirable, pray for us.

Mother of good counsel, pray for us.

Mother of our Creator, pray for us.

Mother of our Savior, pray for us.

Virgin most prudent, pray for us.

Virgin most venerable, pray for us.

Virgin most renowned, pray for us.

Virgin most powerful, pray for us.

Virgin most merciful, pray for us.

Virgin most faithful, pray for us.

Mirror of justice, pray for us.

Seat of wisdom, pray for us.

Cause of our joy, pray for us.

Spiritual vessel, pray for us.

Vessel of honor, pray for us.

Singular vessel of devotion, pray for us.

Mystical rose, pray for us.

Tower of David, pray for us.

Tower of ivory, pray for us.

House of gold, pray for us.

Ark of the covenant, pray for us.

Gate of heaven, pray for us.

Morning star, pray for us.
Health of the sick, pray for us.
Refuge of sinners, pray for us.
Comforter of the afflicted, pray for us.
Help of Christians, pray for us.
Queen of Angels, pray for us.
Queen of Patriarchs, pray for us.
Queen of Prophets, pray for us.
Queen of Apostles, pray for us.
Queen of Martyrs, pray for us.
Queen of Confessors, pray for us.
Queen of Virgins, pray for us.
Queen of all Saints, pray for us.
Queen conceived without original sin, pray for us.
Queen assumed into heaven, pray for us.
Queen of the most holy Rosary, pray for us.
Queen of Peace, pray for us.
Lamb of God, who takest away the sins of the world, spare us, O Lord.
Lamb of God, who takest away the sins of the world, graciously hear us O Lord
Lamb of God, who takest away the sins of the world, have mercy on us.
V. Pray for us, O holy Mother of God.
R. That we may be made worthy of the promises of Christ.

LET US PRAY
Grant, we beseech Thee, O Lord God, unto us Thy servants,
the glorious intercession of Blessed Mary ever Virgin,
may be delivered from present sadness, and enter into the joy
of Thine eternal gladness. Through Christ our Lord. Amen.

—Traditional Marian Devotion

Appendix B
Integrating with *Seton Art 1*

For each book listed below, you will find a corresponding art idea in *Seton Art 1* (page numbers listed reference *Seton Art I*). These are listed in the order they appear in *Catholic Mosaic*.

Mary the Mother of Jesus – use "Mary Holding the Infant Jesus" (see p. 9) and "Presentation of Mary" (see p. 9).

The Last Straw – use "The Wise Men Come" (see p. 9).

A Gift of Gracias – use "The Grotto at Lourdes" (p. 12).

St. Valentine – use "Give Jesus your Heart" (see p. 13).

St. Patrick of Ireland – use "St. Patrick's Day Cards" (see p. 21), and "A Shamrock to Teach the Trinity" (see p. 29).

Song of the Swallows – use "A Stained Glass Window for St. Joseph" (see p. 22).

Hosanna to You, Jesus – use "Palm Sunday" (see p. 16).

The Caterpillar That Finds Jesus and *The Caterpillar That Came to Church* – use "Corpus Christi" (see p. 30).

Lovely Lady Dressed in Blue – use "Mary is Concieved Without Sin" (see p. 4), "Mary Our Mother" (see p. 24), or "A Ribbon of the Seven Sorrows" (see pp. 40-41).

The Weight of a Mass – use "The Eucharist" (see p. 19).

The Tale of Three Trees – use "The Holy Cross" (see p. 42).

My Guardian Dear – use "Make an Advent Angel" (see p.1), "Make a Guardian Angel Prayer Card" (see p.43), or "Make a Stand-up Guardian Angel" (see p. 44).

I Sing a Song of the Saints of God – use "All Saint's Day" (see p. 46).

Father Phillip tells a Ghost Story – use "All Soul's Day" (see p. 47).

Clown of God – use "Christ the King" (see p. 49).

The Donkey's Dream – use "Jesus, Mary, and Joseph Figures" (see p. 7), "Nativity Pop-up" (see p. 5).

Appendix C
Integrating with *A Year with God*

For each book listed below, you will find a corresponding art idea in CHC's *A Year with God* (page numbers listed reference *A Year with God*). These are listed in the order they appear in *Catholic Mosaic*.

Mary the Mother of Jesus – use "Marian Crossword Puzzle"(see p. 55); "Marian Word Search" (see p.65); "Seven Sorrows of Mary" (see p. 200).

The Little Match Girl – use "Spreading the Light of Christ" (see p. 62).

The Last Straw – use "First Benediction" (see pp. 66-67).

A Gift of Gracias – use "Miraculous Medal Craft Idea" (see p. 54).

The Most Beautiful Thing in the World – use "Growing Good Fruit for God" (see pp 110-115).

Patrick, Patron of Ireland – use "Feast of St. Patrick" (see p. 122).

Song of the Swallows – use "Catholic How-to-Draw St. Joseph" (see p.125).

Children's Stations of the Cross – use "Weekly Lenten Calendar" (see p. 104-105).

Little Rose of Sharon – use "Hidden Symbols of the Passion" (see p.107).

Petook – use "My Gifts for Jesus" (see p.106).

The Little Caterpillar That Finds Jesus – use "Solemnity of the Ascension of the Lord" (see pp. 144-145).

The Weight of a Mass – use "Solemnity of the Body and Blood of Christ" (see pp.184-185).

Lady Dressed in Blue – use "Ways Families Celebrate the Month of May" (see pp. 127-128).

Juanita and Our Lady of the Angels – use "Marian Apparition Match-Up" (see p.148).

A Tale of Three Trees – use "Holy Name Match-Up" (see p.199).

Angel in the Waters – use "A Family Effort to Help End Abortion" (see pp.116-117).

My Guardian Dear – use "Feast of the Archangels" (see pp. 201-203).

Father Phillip Tells a Ghost Story – use "All Souls" (see pp. 222-223).

I Sing a Song of the Saints of God – use "Saint Day Activities" (see pp. 77-86, 149-159, 225-249).

The Miracle of St. Nicholas – use "Home Altar" (see pp. 60-61).

The Donkey's Dream – use "Litany of Loreto" (see pp. 56-57); "Litany of Loreto Match-Up" (see pp.194-198).

The Lady of Guadalupe – use "Feast of Our Lady of Guadalupe: A Simple Play" (see pp. 58-59).

The Crippled Lamb – use "Scripture Match-Up" (see p. 63).

Appendix D   ProLife Information

1. Twelve Pro-Life Activities that Anyone Can Do

- Be an example of pro-life through your own family. Family life has been degraded enough. Show through example the strength and well-being of your own family so that others will wish to imitate it.
- Request that your name be added to the pro-life center's prayer line. When the center is experiencing a difficult case in which the mother is determined to go through with an abortion, they put the word out the prayer line to pray for this mother and her unborn child. When a call comes in for extra prayers, instruct your prayer warriors to take out their secret weapon—the rosary—and pray.
- Go to garage sales and pick up baby items to donate to the pro-life center.
- Volunteer a few hours a month at a nearby center to sort and stack newborn clothing. Folding these little outfits and sleepers is the best way to refresh your sense of commitment to the pro-life movement.
- Make little care packets or baskets containing baby necessities (baby lotion, powder, pacifier, comb and brush set) for the new mothers at the counseling centers. Add pro-life literature to these kits.
- Make sure your church is regularly putting pro-life inserts in its Sunday bulletin.
- Write letters to your senators and congressmen. Don't ask them for their pro-life support; tell them what can happen without it. For politicians who support pro-life, remember to thank them for their efforts. They are used to complaints. They will be appreciative of a thank-you.
- Stay informed of pro-life news and arguments. You may find yourself in a group of anti-lifers, and the best way to sway their convictions is not to argue with them but to speak the truth.
- Keep praying. Each month adopt a mother and an unborn child to pray for. This may seem like the smallest, easiest thing to do, but its impact is the greatest. Nothing is accomplished without prayer and God's grace.
- Pray a pro-life rosary
- Visit a nursing home
- Offer to read pro-life books like *Angel in the Waters* and *Horton Hears a Who* to elementary CCD classes.

2. Spiritual Adoption of a Baby

This activity is described in the study guide for *Angel in the Waters*. The child adopts a baby for whom to pray for nine months. The child can decorate and color this card and laminate it if possible. Since he/she may not know the baby's name, give it a saint's name and ask that saint to pray as well. In the blank space above the baby's name, place a small holy card or an image of a guardian angel. We have included one, but you should encourage your child to select one himself/herself.

Spiritual
Adoption
Card

Baby's Name

_____

I will pray for nine months

from _____ (month)

until _____ (month).

3. A Child's Respect for Life Day

This may be done when reading *Angel in the Waters* or *Lovely Lady Dressed in Blue*.

There is an increasing need in today's world to teach our children a fervent, healthy respect for life. This cannot take place in a structured classroom setting. It can only be taught in the home by loving, concerned parents who show love and respect for their children.

To pass on a respect for life message to our children, we must become consciously aware of life in our daily routine. One way to help nourish this attitude in our children is to start with a "Respect for Life Day." Choose a day, any day—tomorrow, this weekend, the anniversary of your child's Baptism—and implement a "life" message into everything you do that day.

Breakfast: At the breakfast table, open the curtains so that your children get a good view of the yard. Have them point out signs of life: a bird, a budding tree, a near-by squirrel.

Brushing Teeth: Have each child look at his/her reflection in the mirror. To reinforce the message that your child is a unique human being, reflect with him about his eyes (to see with), his ears (to hear with), his nose (to smell with), etc. Remind the child how blessed he is to have the gift of these senses from God.

Exercise: Dance to music, act silly. Then have your children rest on the floor. Once the giggling and talking have quieted down, remind your children that some children are too sick or do not have arms or legs to do exercises. Tell your children that every human person is a child of God. Our goodness does not depend on what we look like or what we can do, but on the special love God has for each person.

Lunch: Pack a picnic lunch if it's a pretty day. Go for a walk and take note of God's creation. As you eat, talk to your children about why the body needs good food. Our bodies are the temple of the Holy Spirit and we must take care of our bodies by eating healthy food.

Visit a maternity ward: Children love to see newborn babies. If you have a maternity ward at a nearby hospital, visit it and, while viewing the babies, say a quiet prayer for these newest children of God.

Go to a garage sale: As you leave the hospital, tell your children that there are some women who are still carrying their babies inside of them that are too poor to buy clothes for the baby when it's born. Ask your children if they would like to help these women. Find a garage sale or thrift store that has baby clothes and let the children pick some out to buy. If you have a crisis pregnancy center in or near your town, bring the clothes there. Tell your children how the center helps mothers who need assistance. Ask the center if they have the little 12-week fetus models and get one for each child.

Visit a nursing home: This visit may bother your child if he or she is not use to elderly people, but it is an opportunity to show your children that respect for life must extend to the sick and elderly as well as little babies. Tell them how God thinks life is precious in all stages because He made each of us and loves us always. Elderly people usually love to have young children visit. Let your children talk to them and mingle with them. As you leave, tell your children how many of the people in the nursing home have children and grandchildren. Tell them how these people could tell marvelous stories about when they were little boys and girls. This helps your children to realize that these people were young once and had families. It enhances the message that the elderly are a part of "life" and must always be respected.

Feed the pets: Before concluding the day, have the children feed their pets. This may be a job that daddy usually does every evening when he gets in from work. Help your children scoop the food for the dog, sprinkle the fish food onto the water, or give a slice of apple to the hamster. As you feed and water your pet, talk to your children about how we must respect all God's creation. He has given us animals to be our friends. We must not neglect or be cruel to them but take care of them and love them. Tell them the story about St. Francis of Assisi and his love for animals.

Bathtime: Ask your children if they have something they wish could be changed about themselves (a mole, a birthmark, funny ears). Do *not* point things out. The way children view themselves at a young age must be handled sensitively. Let your child think of something. Then discuss God's love for us no matter our appearance.

Quiet time: It has been a busy day. Lay in bed with your children snuggled along side of you. Show pictures of them as babies. Tell them each about the day of their birth and how happy you were that day.

Bedtime prayers: Tuck your children into bed and get the fetus models they received at the clinic (pictures of a developing baby also work well). Point out how well-developed the baby is in such a short time. Tell your child that the fetus model represents a tiny unborn baby. With your child, say a prayer for the unborn and for expectant mothers. Then add, for your child to hear, your own prayer of thanksgiving for the blessing of the child next to you.

Appendix E – Outline Maps

You may use these maps to add a geographic element to your literature study. Hang the map of the world on the wall and place a dot for the location of each story. Each child may also have his or her own copy of the world map for marking up. Some of the individual books guides in the Mosaic ask the student to find something on a map. After using an atlas, (online resource www.worldatlas.com), the student may color or fill in his own map.

These maps are used by permission of www.worldatlas.com and may be reproduced for your home use. Many more maps of individual countries can be found at this website.

Used by permission www.worldatlas.com

Map of Central America

A Gift of Gracias – Dominican Republic
Juanita and Our Lady of the Angels – Costa Rica

Used by permission www.worldatlas.com

Map of Costa Rica

Used by permission www.worldatlas.com

Map of Europe

(next page)

St. Patrick, Patron Saint of Ireland
St. Brigid's Cloak – Ireland
Across a Dark and Wild Sea, St. Columcille – Ireland (and Scotland)
Mother Teresa (joined Sisters of Loreto) – Ireland
Blackbird's Nest, a Tale of St. Kevin – Ireland
Karol from Poland
Mother Teresa (born in Macedonia)
The Holy Twins, St. Benedict and St. Scholastica – Italy
Good Man of Assisi, St. Francis – Italy
St. Valentine – Italy
Brother Joseph, Painter of Icons (referencing Fra Angelico) – Italy
Lovely Lady Dressed in Blue – France

235

Map of Ireland

St. Patrick, Patron Saint of Ireland
St. Brigid' Cloak – Ireland
Across a Dark and Wild Sea, St. Columcille – Ireland (and Scotland)
Mother Teresa (joined Sisters of Loreto) – Ireland
Blackbird's Nest, a Tale of St. Kevin – Ireland

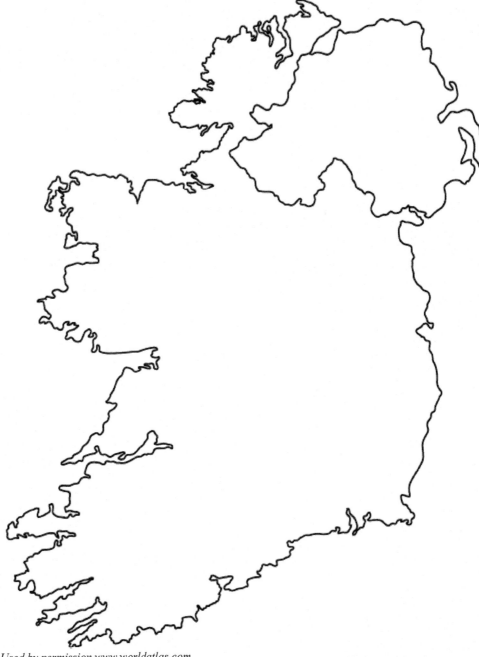

Used by permission www.worldatlas.com

Map of Italy

The Holy Twins, St. Benedict and St. Scholastica
Good Man of Assisi, St. Francis
St. Valentine
Brother Joseph, Painter of Icons (referencing Fra Angelico)

Map of California

Song of the Swallows

Used by permission www.worldatlas.com

Map of Africa

A Saint and his Lion, A Tale of St. Tekla

Map of Mexico

Spirit of Tio Fernando
Our Lady of Guadalupe

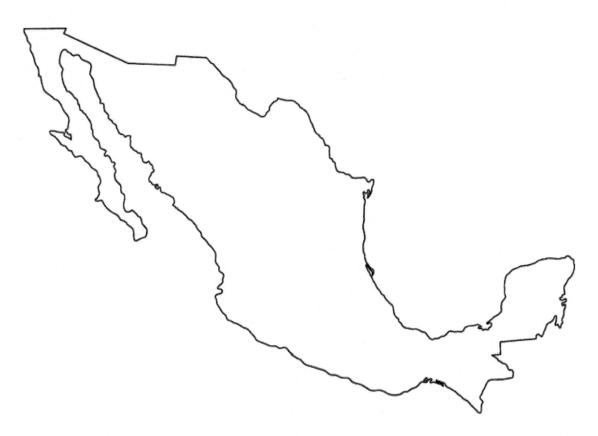

Used by permission www.worldatlas.com

Map of South America

Peter Claver, Patron Saint of Slaves – Cartagena, Colombia

Used by permission www.worldatlas.com
Map of Colombia http://worldatlas.com/webimage/countrys/samerica/outline/coout.htm

Map of Asia

(turned sideways)

Miracle of St. Nicholas – Russia

Mother Teresa – India

CPSIA information can be obtained
at www.ICGtesting.com
Printed in the USA
BVOW10s0811310716

457436BV00014B/276/P